CLASSIC
GOLF

Created by the Top That! Team
Consultant: Stephen Whymark

TOP THAT!
Copyright © 2004 Top That! Publishing Inc,
25031 W. Avenue Stanford, Suite #60, Valencia, CA 91355.
All rights reserved.
www.topthatpublishing.com

CONTENTS

Introduction	4	Toeing	56
History & Development	6	Topping	58
Equipment	10	Shanking	60
Clothing	14	Thin & Fat Shots	62
Choosing Your Clubs	16	**IMPROVING YOUR SCORE**	64
THE BASICS	18	Shaping Shots	66
Gripping the Club	20	Getting Backspin	74
Alignment	22	Adapting to Conditions	76
Posture	24	Setting Goals	78
Pre-Shot Routine	26	Fitness & Warming Up	80
Putting	28	Practicing Your Long Game	82
Swing – Backswing	32	Practicing Your Short Game	86
Swing – Downswing	34	Practicing Your Putting	90
Swing – Follow-through	36	Mental Strength	94
Chipping	38	Course Management	96
Pitching	40	**ON THE COURSE**	100
From the Sand Trap	42	The Handicap System	102
Playing From Poor Lies	44	Types of Competition	104
From the Rough	46	Rules of Golf	106
FAULT CLINIC	48	Etiquette	110
Slice	50	Records	114
Hook	52	Tournaments and Champions	118
Skying	54	Glossary	122

INTRODUCTION

Welcome to Classic Golf, your complete guide to this wonderful game. Whether you're thinking of taking up the sport, or if you already play and want to improve your score, this book provides the essential advice for you to get the most out of the game.

Mark Twain famously said that golf was a good walk spoiled, but today there are millions of people who would disagree with him. The beauty of the game is that it combines wonderful views, some gentle exercise and the opportunity for a little friendly competition. It's no wonder that so many people who take up the game get the "golf bug"— that desire to play as often as possible.

The first section covers the basics. It is worth studying this section however long you've been playing because it is easy to develop bad habits without realizing. A good golfer will review their grip and swing regularly.

No matter how good a player you are there will be times when you play badly. The Fault Clinic will help you keep those times to a minimum.

If you want to play competitively, Improving Your Score will give you the edge over your rivals as the advice given will ensure that you trim a few shots from your round.

If you've played a few rounds and have got the bug, you'll want to read the final section to immerse yourself in the things that make golf truly unique – its etiquette and rules.

But that's not all. We've also included tees, ball markers, a towel, a divot repairer and a scorecard holder to set you on your way.

HISTORY & DEVELOPMENT

Despite its modest beginnings, today golf is one of the most internationally popular sports.

The Early Years

First played in Scotland in the early fifteenth century, players would hit a pebble with a primitive club into a hole. The game's popularity grew rapidly but was stopped in its tracks in 1457 when King James II banned the sport because his countrymen were spending too much time playing and not enough preparing for military action . However, the ban was lifted in 1502 and the game was on its way to global domination.

The Nineteenth Century

The Industrial Revolution helped the game's growth nationally, as railways made it easier for people to travel longer distances and get to the golf courses sprouting up across the British countryside. The game's popularity was confirmed by the holding of the first national championship, at Prestwick, Scotland in 1860.

International growth meanwhile was, in part, fostered by the existence of the British Empire, which gave Britain some cultural influence abroad and led directly to the building of golf courses in Commonwealth countries.

However, the game was also growing in America despite the absence of significant British influence. By the end of the century there were 1,000 courses in the US and a magazine for enthusiasts, *Golf*, had begun publication in 1897.

The Twentieth Century

Several factors have contributed to the game's growth in the twentieth century. Improved transport made international tournaments truly viable, television has transmitted the game to a huge audience and the rise of leisure as an industry, driven by the increasing amount of leisure time, has seen the number of golfers increase dramatically. But it is not just external factors that have driven the game's growth.

By putting on set piece events such as the Ryder Cup, the US Open, the US Masters, the US PGA and the British Open, golf's masters have created interest in the game. In turn this has made more people interested, forced prices down and made the game increasingly affordable.

Technology

Both clubs and balls have changed dramatically since the game began. Early clubs were handcrafted and balls were made of goose feather and leather.

In the nineteenth century gutta percha balls and hickory shafts were introduced but they have been supplanted with graphite shafts and two or three-piece rubber-cored balls which are now the most common.

Today's technology is so advanced that the best golfers can hit the ball over 300 yards with titanium clubs and balls can be manufactured to suit a particular player's game.

KEY DATES

1457	King James II of Scotland bans game.
1502	Treaty of Glasgow lifts ban.
1618	Golf ball introduced. It is made of goose feathers and leather.
1764	World's first 18-hole golf course, St Andrews, Scotland, opens.
1826	Hickory shaft introduced.
1848	Gutta percha (rubber) balls manufactured.
1860	First national championship, held at Prestwick, Scotland.
1894	USGA formed to regulate the game in US and Mexico.
1895	First US Open held at Newport, Rhode Island.
1897	First magazine on sport, *Golf*, published.
1898	One-piece rubber-cored ball introduced.
c.1900	Persimmon shaft introduced.
1902	Groove-faced irons introduced.
1905	Dimpled ball invented.
1916	PGA of America formed and first US PGA Championship played.
1927	First official Ryder Cup.
1934	First US Masters played at Augusta, Florida.
1961	US PGA withdraws whites-only rule from constitution.
1963	Club heads made by casting iron.
1972	Two-piece rubber-cored ball introduced.
1973	Graphite shaft introduced.
1979	Ryder Cup extended to include European players.

EQUIPMENT

Clubs

Clubs are divided into drivers and woods, irons, wedges and a putter. There are five woods (ranging from the driver to the 5-wood), nine irons, (ranging from the 1-iron to the 9-iron), four wedges (pitching, sand, gap and lob) and the putter. Drivers and woods are used for tee shots and long fairway shots, irons for shorter tee shots and off the fairway—the lower the number you are using the greater the distance the ball will travel. Wedges are used when you are near to the green and the putter is for knocking the ball in the hole when you get there. You are not allowed more than fourteen clubs in your bag so most players will only carry four woods, seven irons, two wedges and a putter. Today you will find woods are usually made of metal composites.

Bag

Trolleys can be hired if you don't want to carry your bag of clubs. Cart bags are designed to fit on a cart, or golf buggy, while stand bags have legs to keep the bag upright when you put it down.

Spiked shoes

Many golf courses will insist that you wear spiked shoes as these reduce the damage to the greens. They come in two types, metal and soft-spiked. Soft spikes, made of a rubbery material, are preferable because they are easier on the feet and are less damaging to the green.

Balls

There are many different balls available, some will travel further through the air while others will offer greater accuracy. The main thing to remember is to find a ball that suits you and the course you play most often and then always use that type.

Glove

For a right-hander the glove should be worn on the left hand. The use of a glove is not essential, but it will protect against blisters and other skin problems.

Towel
Included in the kit, use this to keep your ball clean.

Head Covers
These are not absolutely necessary but you can use them to protect the club heads of your woods from wear and tear.

Divot Repairer
Included in the kit, this should be used on the green. If, when your ball lands, it makes an indentation in the grass, then the divot must be repaired to minimise damage to the green.

Tees
Included in the kit, these are used to raise the ball by about an inch for the first shot at each hole. They can only be used for the first shot.

Ball Markers
Included in the kit, these are used on the green. Golf etiquette dictates that the player whose ball is furthest from the hole plays first. Therefore, if your ball is in the way you should mark the spot with a ball marker and then pick the ball up.

Scorecard
Whenever you play, you will be issued with a scorecard. You should enter your score for each hole as soon as you have played it. To make life easier, a scorecard holder is included in the kit.

CLOTHING

Although plus fours are no longer de rigueur, golf courses require certain standards of dress. In general, jeans and T-shirts are not permitted.

Men
Men should wear trousers, a shirt with a collar and golf shoes. Shorts that reach below the knee are often acceptable.

Women
Women should wear trousers or knee-length shorts, a shirt with a collar and golf shoes.

Be Practical
It's important to wear clothes that aren't too tight as these will restrict your movement when executing a shot. If the weather's good you should wear light clothes to keep you as cool as possible. Also take a visor or dark glasses, a hat and sunscreen to protect you from the sun's rays. If it's windy, wear clothes which will protect you against it, and if it looks like it might rain, make sure that you have some waterproof clothing in your bag.

Most bags will have an umbrella holder, so it's no inconvenience to carry one and you'll be grateful for it if the rain starts coming down. But if there's a chance of lightning you should leave the course immediately as your clubs may leave you in danger of being electrocuted.

CHOOSING YOUR CLUBS

What to Consider

When buying clubs the two most important things to consider are the length of the clubs and the grip size. You will not be able to play to the best of your ability if your clubs are too small, or if the grip is incorrect for you. If you're taking lessons, get your coach to advise you on which clubs will best suit you.

For the more advanced player looking for a replacement set, swing weight, lie angle and type of shaft will also be important factors to consider.

Starting Out

If you're just starting out, it is probably not worth your while buying a brand new full set of clubs. Look in your local paper or golf magazines where you will find plenty of advertisements for secondhand clubs. Try these first and wait until you "get the bug" before making that big investment.

Another option is to buy a half-set. This will include four irons, a wedge, a putter and a couple of woods.

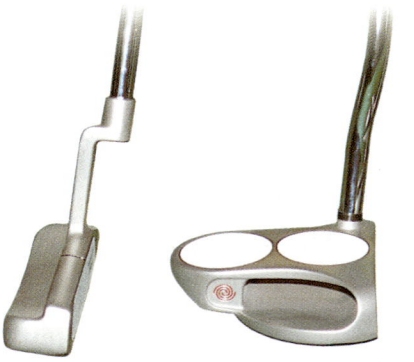

Where to Look
Your local golf course will almost certainly have a shop with a good selection of sets available. This may not always be the cheapest option but the shop's staff will probably be keen players and the expert advice you will receive will be invaluable in the long term.

THE BASICS

To play golf to the maximum of your ability it is critical that you get the basics right. This will give your game a sound basis from which to progress.

It will be worth your while grooving your game because the better you play the more you will enjoy being out on the course. However, studying the basics is not just for beginners. Even if you have been playing for a long time it is likely that some elementary errors have crept into your game.

As with vehicles, your game needs to be serviced regularly. Checking your grip, swing, alignment and posture every three months or so will ensure your technique remains in good order. Time spent practicing off the course will be amply rewarded when you play for real.

The instructions that follow are for the right-hander but are equally valid for the left-hander, as long as they use the opposite arm or leg, where applicable.

GRIPPING THE CLUB

Grip is critical to your success as a golfer. Holding the club correctly will help you to hit the ball straight and also to generate more power.

1. Hold the club in your left hand, towards the top of the grip. The thumb should point down the club towards the club face.

2. Hold the club out in front of you, at an angle of about 45 degrees.

3. Put your right hand on the club, roughly where the grip meets the shaft. Then, slide the fingers of your right hand towards your left hand until they meet.

4. Interlock your hands by putting the little finger of your right hand between the forefinger and middle finger of your left hand.

5. Check that the thumbs of both hands are pointing directly down the club. The two knuckles of your left hand should be visible.

6. Make sure your grip is not too tight. It is better to hold it lightly as your hands will naturally grip more tightly as you swing.

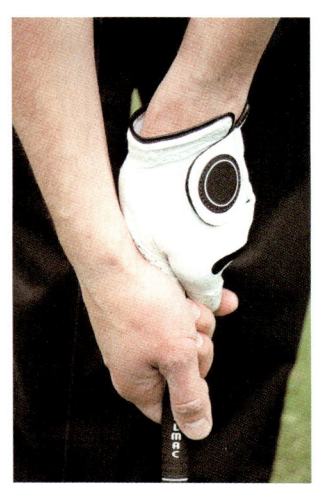

ALIGNMENT

The key to good alignment is to line up your feet, hips and shoulders parallel to the target. Remember, it is the club head that should be aiming at the target, not the player.

1. Stand directly behind your ball and decide on your target. You should pick out a spot between your ball and the target but nearer your ball.

2. Lay the club on the ground between ball and target, aiming it at this intermediate marker.

3. Take two more clubs and place them parallel and on either side of the first club. Each club should be a club length apart. Now remove the center club.

4. Line up your feet, hips and shoulders with the club on your left.

Remember, you can only do this on the practice ground. Start doing it on the course and you'll be in trouble for slow play.

POSTURE

As you may be beginning to realize, successful golf is about putting all the disparate functions together to make a fluent whole.

Although the position of the ball between your feet will vary depending on what shot you are playing and how the ball is lying, the basic posture will remain the same.

1. Stand up straight.

2. Bend your back forwards, but keeping it straight.

3. Flex your knees and then settle your weight on your heels.

PRE-SHOT ROUTINE

Giving yourself a pre-shot routine will help you to focus on the shot you have to play.

1. Stand behind your ball and pick out the target you are going to aim at.

2. Assess the wind and the dryness of the ground as both will affect how far your ball will travel.

3. Make a mental picture of the shot you intend to play.

4. Once you have decided which club you are going to use stay with it. If you're in two minds over which club to take, you are likely to play a poor shot because of the doubt in your mind, not because you took the wrong club.

5. Take a practice swing, but if you're preparing a tee shot, this should be taken well away from the tee itself.

6. Address the ball. With the club in your right hand, move from behind the ball to the left and line up the club as described in Alignment (pages 22–23).

7. Now grip the club as described in Gripping the Club (pages 20–21).

8. Before you swing, look at the target once more.

9. If something disturbs you during your routine start the process again.

PUTTING

You may be surprised that putting appears at this stage of the book but there's a sound reason for it.

The putting stroke requires the shortest swing of the club so you should master it before moving your arms in a wider arc for longer shots. But there is more to putting than a good swing and you need to get all the elements right to make sure your ball drops into the hole.

Swing
The arms, hands and shoulders should move together in unison. The length of the putt will dictate the extent of the swing.

Grip
Although you may wish to use the grip described in Gripping the Club (pages 20–21) many golfers will use a different style for putting – one that helps to produce a pendulum style and thus greater accuracy.

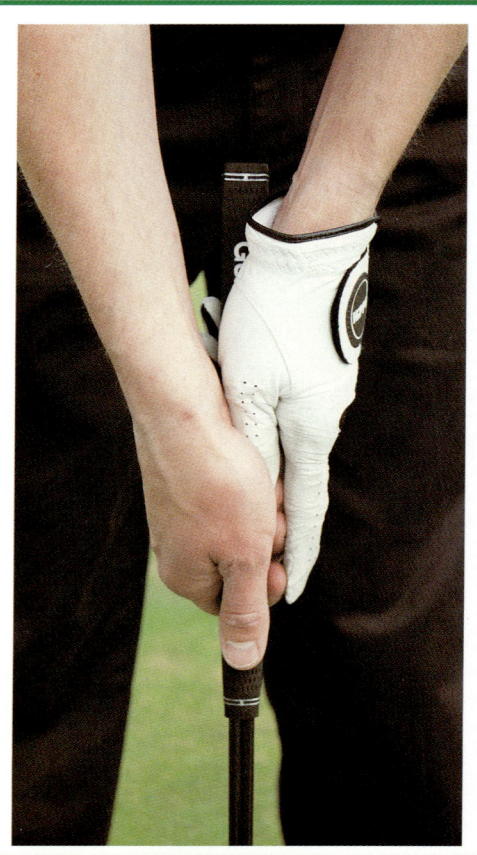

1. Holding the putter in your left hand, put your middle, third and left finger around the grip.

2. Point your left thumb down the club.

3. Put your right hand on the club, placing the little finger on the middle finger of your left hand.

4. Position your left forefinger so that it points downwards across the fingers of your right hand.

Alignment
1. Position your feet, hips and shoulder parallel to the target. The ball should be just behind your left foot.

2. Your dominant eye should be directly over the ball.

Reading the Green

Putting from anything more than a few feet away from the hole is unlikely to be a question of hitting the ball in a straight line and judging the weight correctly. The contours of the green will make your ball deviate on its way to the hole.

First, check that there is no debris between your ball and the hole as you are allowed to remove it. Then kneel behind your ball and look at the ground carefully. If there are contours severe enough to affect your ball's journey make sure you account for them in your aiming of the ball.

The Stroke

Swing the club in a straight line. The backswing and the follow-through should travel the same distance. It's easy to fall into the trap of pushing the club at the ball rather than swinging through but this should be avoided as you will lose accuracy and control of the weight of the stroke. Neither should you follow the ball with your eyes until you have completed your follow-through. By doing so you will open your shoulders, sending the ball off target.

SWING – BACKSWING

A correct backswing will help you gain power and accuracy while a faulty one could see you in the deep rough searching for your ball.

1. Decide how far back you intend to take the club. This will depend on how far you want to hit the ball. Sometimes players will take the club so far back that the club head has gone over the right shoulder and the club head is in front of them.

However, the further you take the club back in your backswing the harder it is to control and you should never sacrifice control in a bid for more power. On other occasions it will only be necessary to take the club back to waist height.

2. Take the club away from the ball slowly. Your hands, arms and shoulders should form a triangle that moves with the club.

3. Make sure that you turn your shoulders as this will help you to generate power.

4. When you reach the top of the backswing hold the position for a split second before beginning the downswing. This will help you to control the downswing without losing any power.

5. Throughout the backswing try to keep your head as still as possible and over the ball as this will also help you to retain control.

SWING – DOWNSWING

A good backswing will be wasted unless it is followed by a good downswing. Resist the urge to rush the downswing, as a fluid action will generate much greater power, control and accuracy.

1. Maintaining the triangle of hands, arms and shoulders, bring the club down towards the ball.

2. There is no real need to execute the downswing slowly. If you've got the backswing right you should be able to bring the club head down at great speed, unleashing the power you want to generate. But remember, if you are accelerating the swing faster than you can control it, you will play a bad shot.

3. As with the backswing, you should try to keep your head as still as possible, with your eyes focused on the ball.

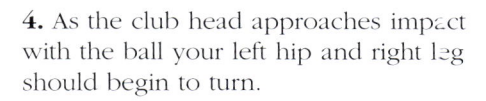

4. As the club head approaches impact with the ball your left hip and right leg should begin to turn.

SWING – FOLLOW-THROUGH

The key to a good follow-through is to maintain the fluid movement you built up with your backswing and downswing.

1. Your stroke goes from downswing to follow-through upon impact with the ball. You should allow the momentum generated by your body to carry through the ball.

2. You should continue to follow through until the club head is over your left shoulder, your left hip and right leg have turned and you are facing the direction in which you hit the ball.

3. Your finished position should be controlled. If you are unable to balance, elements of your swing will be at fault; poor weight transfer will be the prime suspect! If this is the case it is a good idea to practice your swing with your feet close together. This will help you to prevent excessive movement in your swing and encourage better weight transfer.

When you've got the backswing, the downswing and the follow-through in good working order you'll have the complete action. Study the pictures below to check that you have got the actions right. Strive for a fluid movement from the top of the backswing to the end of the follow-through.

CHIPPING

Chipping is for shots close to the green when you want the ball to run on towards the hole.

The club to use will depend on how much loft you need to achieve. A sand wedge or lob wedge will give you most height but there may be situations when you want to keep the ball as low as possible, in which case a low iron will be appropriate. You are unlikely to want to chip the ball if you are more than 40 yards from the hole when pitching will probably be the better option.

1. Put your feet close together and position your hips and shoulders square to the ball.

2. Ensure that the ball is to the back of the stance, ideally virtually opposite your right foot.

3. Hold the club lower down the grip.

4. Cock your hands so the grip of the club is ahead of the ball.

5. Pick the spot where you want the ball to land. You want your ball to finish on the green so you need to consider how far it is likely to roll after it lands.

PITCHING

Pitching is the technique to use when you are placed 70 to 40 yards from the hole. Top players will aim to take no more than two shots to get their ball into the hole from this distance and you should aim to take no more than three.

The key is to get your pitch as near to the hole as you can so as to make your putt as easy as possible. Depending on the distance, the club you use will be either a lob wedge, sand wedge or pitching wedge.

1. Stand with your legs slightly closer together than you would for a longer shot.

2. Position your legs so that the ball is in the middle of your stance.

3. Cock your hands so that they are slightly ahead of the ball.

4. Visualize the shot you wish to play. The higher you can hit the ball, the less it will roll when it lands, giving you more control of the ball's finishing point.

5. Swing through the shot as you would normally. The extent of your swing will be dictated by the power you can generate, but make sure that the backswing and follow-through are of equal length.

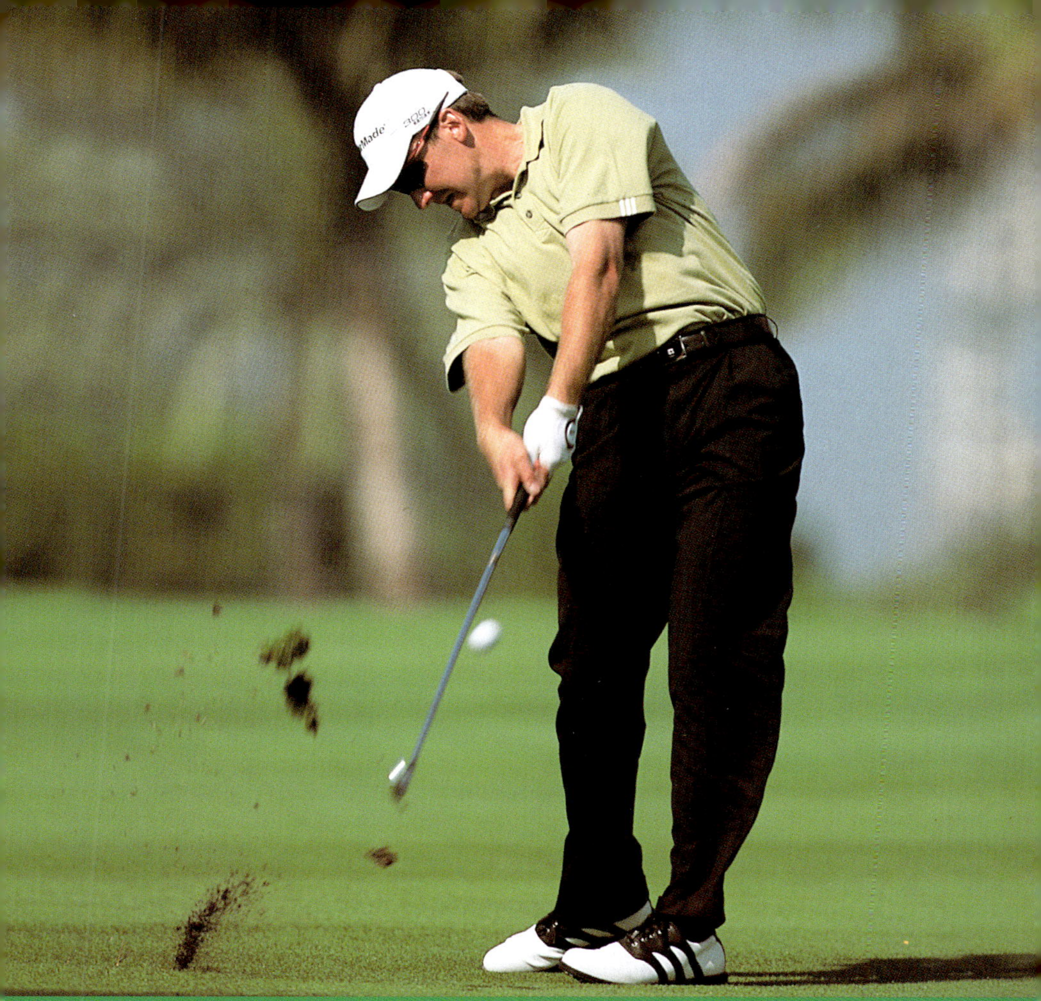

FROM THE SAND TRAP

Finding yourself in the sand trap does not necessarily mean you've played a bad shot. The well-struck shot can be foiled by a swirling wind or an unfortunate kick off the fairway. Sand trap play is therefore an essential skill to practice.

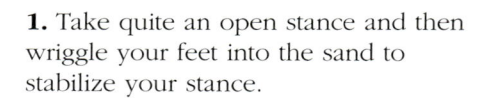

1. Take quite an open stance and then wriggle your feet into the sand to stabilize your stance.

2. Set the club face to the right of the target before taking your grip as this will help you to get more height. Bear in mind that you are not allowed to touch the sand with your club before you play the stroke.

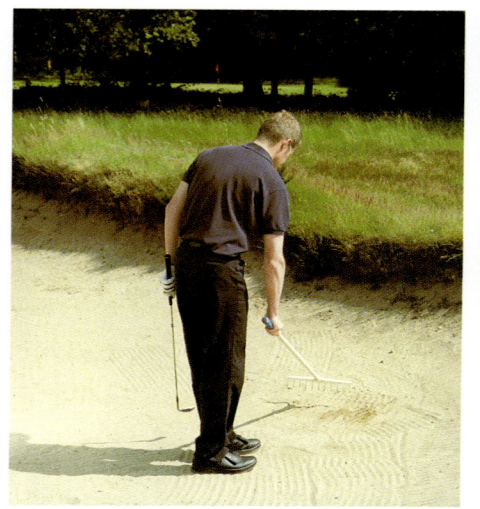

3. Set your body to the left of the target, to offset the fact that you are aiming the clubface to the right.

4. Although the ball is in the middle of your stance your swing should take you through the sand a couple of inches behind the ball. The ball should be lifted out on a bed of sand.

5. Swing through the club as you would normally, but snap your wrists early in the backswing to help you gain height.

6. Remain positive. It is easy to fall into the trap of pulling out of the follow-through because you are worried the ball is going to travel miles past the target. But if you don't follow through properly you will not get any lift and will have to play a second shot from the sand.

7. For the benefit of players behind you, rake the sand trap after your shot.

PLAYING FROM POOR LIES

You will often find your ball lying awkwardly on the fairway. Although the basics remain the same, these tips should help.

Uphill Slope
1. Select a lower-numbered iron ("take one more club") for the shot than you would if the ball was lying flat. This will ensure a lower trajectory to compensate for the slope.

2. Your ball should be positioned slightly nearer to your left foot.

3. Concentrate your weight on your right side.

Downhill Slope
1. Take one less club to ensure a higher trajectory.

2. The ball should be positioned to the back of your stance.

3. Concentrate your weight on your left side.

Ball Above Feet
1. Stand up straighter than you normally would.

2. Aim more to the right to avoid hooking the ball.

Ball Below Feet
1. Crouch down to compensate for the position of the ball.

2. Aim more to the left to avoid slicing the ball.

Divots
1. Take one more club than if the ball was lying well.

2. The ball should be positioned to the back of your stance.

3. Cock your hands so that they are slightly ahead of the ball.

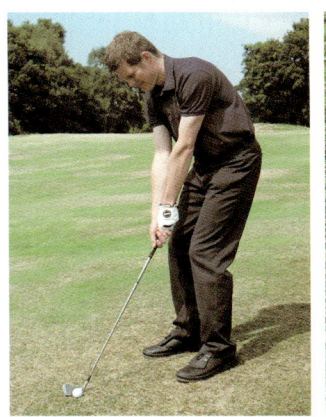

FROM THE ROUGH

Trouble on the golf course comes in many different forms but the hardest place to play from is the rough. Stay out of it if you can and if you're in it get out as quickly as possible.

The shot you play will be dictated by the lie of the ball. If you're fortunate and the ball is lying well you can probably play the same shot as you would on the fairway. But if it's lying badly you'll need to make some adjustments.

1. Use one of the high irons. You've got to get the ball into the air if you're to get it out of the rough.

2. You may have problems getting a good stance so take time to get your balance right.

3. The ball should be positioned in the middle of your stance.

4. Take as little of the grass behind the ball as possible as you need to try and get a clean strike.

5. Be conservative when setting your target. The key is to make sure you get the ball out of the rough. Don't go for an ambitious distance that you only have a 50-50 chance of making.

6. Remain confident as you swing through the ball. You may hit a lot of debris after impact so you need to hold the club quite tightly to keep your follow-through correct.

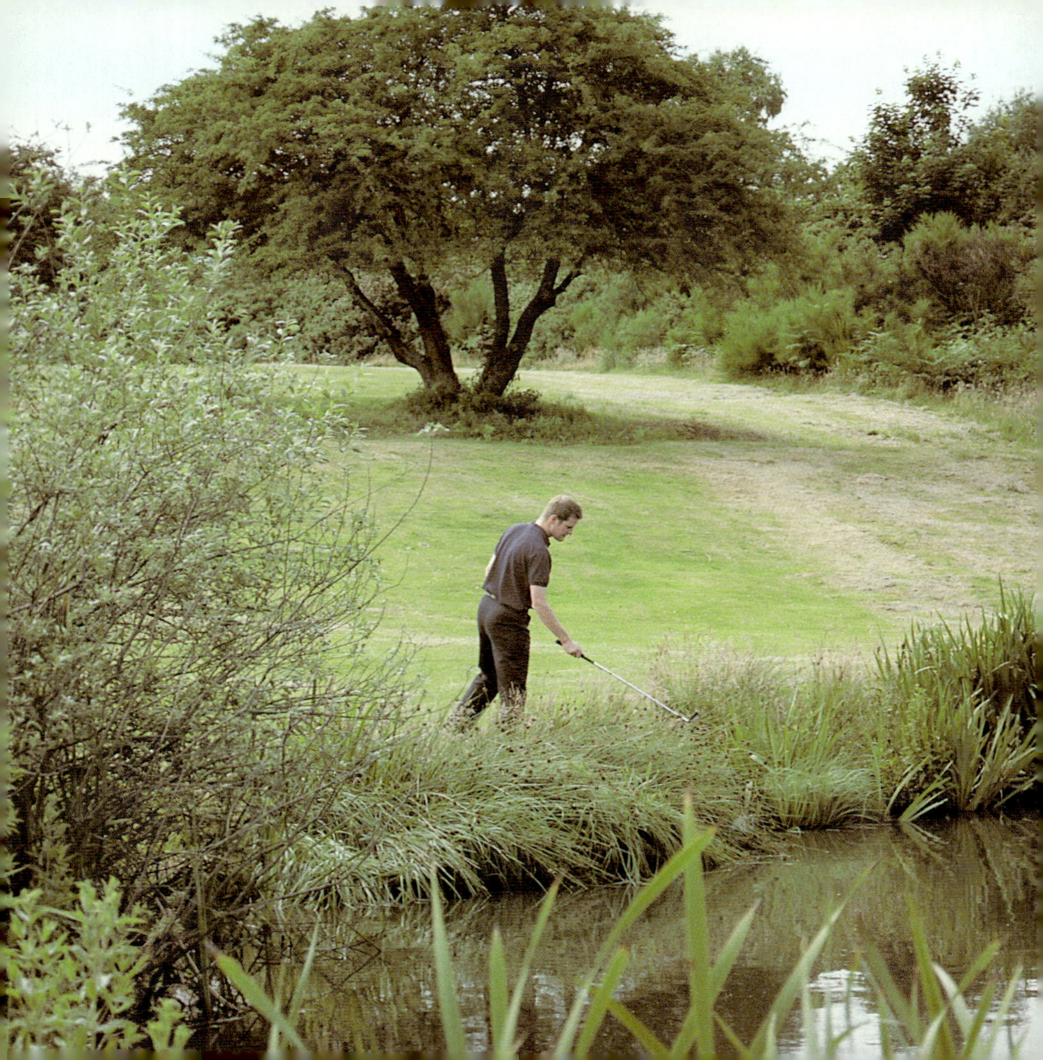

FAULT CLINIC

No matter how good you are, you are sure to play one or two bad shots each round. However, playing the same bad shot repeatedly suggests you have developed a bad habit!

In golf there are many ways of hitting a shot badly. Slicing, hooking, skying, pulling, pushing, toeing and topping are all problems best avoided.

The golf course will invariably punish poor shots. You'll find yourself in the rough, a sand trap or even a water trap. Even if you're lucky enough not to have lost your ball, you'll still have a tricky shot.

It is more effective to cure faults on the practice ground, so take some balls and iron out the problem there before returning to the course itself. Focus on the shot that has been going wrong, analyze the problem and keep hitting balls until you are repeatedly striking the ball well.

SLICE

If you're slicing or pulling the ball the problem almost certainly lies with the arc of your swing as the club is traveling from the right of the ball to its left on impact. There are a variety of possible reasons for this.

Likely causes
1. The ball is positioned too far forward in the stance.

2. Your posture is poor, restricting the movement in your shoulders.

3. You are gripping too tight on the club.

Cures
1. Position the ball further back in your stance.

2. Check that your shoulders are aligned to the right, allowing the club to come in a smooth arc rather than moving from right to left.

3. Check your grip, making sure you can see at least two knuckles on your top hand.

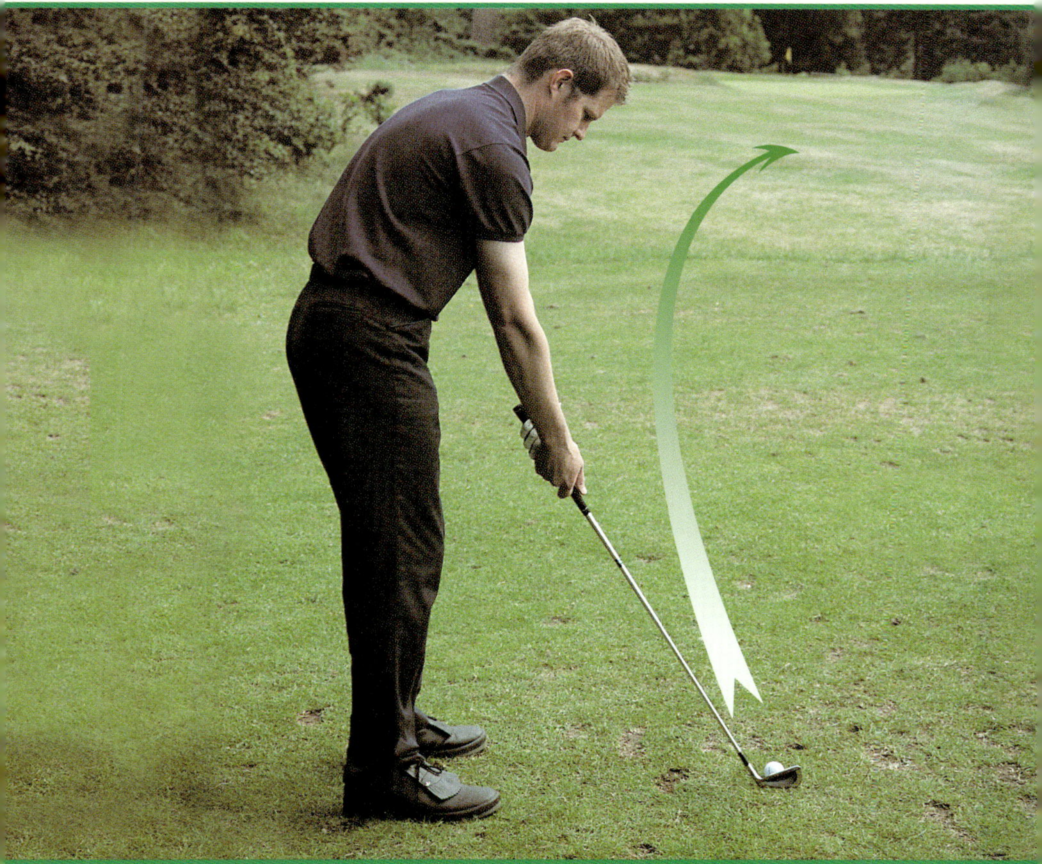

HOOK

If you are hooking or pushing the ball with woods and long irons you may find that the ball is still traveling in a straight line when using the shorter irons.

Unfortunately, this doesn't mean that the problem only lies with your long iron shots. It's simply the case that more lofted clubs make allowances for this.

The basic problem is that you are closing the club face on impact with the ball.

Likely Causes
1. The grip is too tight.

2. The ball is positioned too far back in the stance.

3. You are aiming too far to the right.

4. The swing arc is wrong with the club face coming down on the ball's left before striking it on the right.

5. The swing is slowing down as the club face and ball approach impact.

Cures
1. Check your grip by referring to Gripping the Club (pages 20–21).

2. Make sure the ball is positioned much further forward in your stance, ideally opposite your front foot.

3. Check that you are aligned correctly with your shoulders square on to the ball.

4. Keep your swing fluent, with no change of pace from the top of the downswing to the end of the follow-through. This will help to ensure that your body rotates correctly.

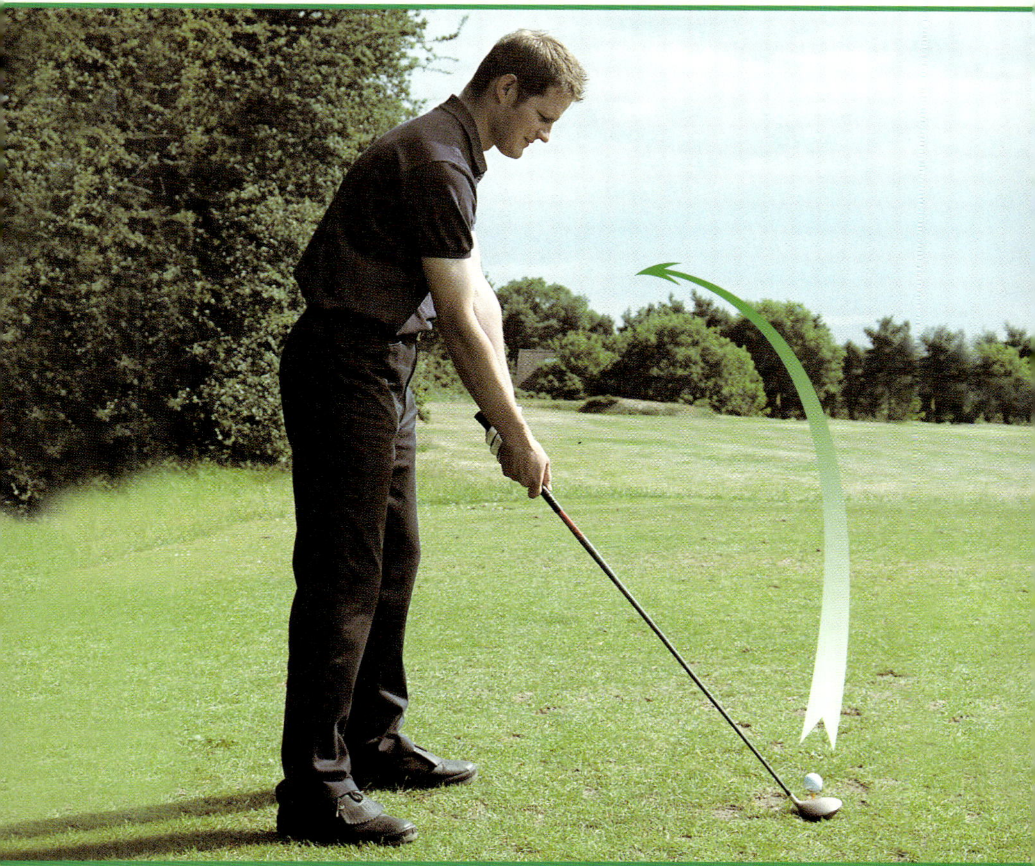

SKYING

Although you are unlikely to sky the ball very often it is very annoying when it happens. What starts as a promising high-reaching shot soon disappoints when the ball plummets, landing only half the expected distance away. The basic problem is that you have hit the ball too far below its center.

Likely Causes

1. Teeing the ball up too high.

2. Too much weight on the left foot.

3. The swing arc is wrong because the club has been pulled up too sharply at the beginning of the backswing.

4. You have tried to hit the ball as hard as you can and consequently created problems by rushing your swing.

Cures

1. Put your tee lower into the ground. However, if you are skying the ball regularly, it is unlikely that the height of the tee is the problem.

2. Make sure that your weight is evenly distributed.

3. Keep your swing smooth. Bear in mind that the club face must approach the ball parallel to the ground for a few inches before impact. You do not need to try and scoop the ball in order to get it in the air.

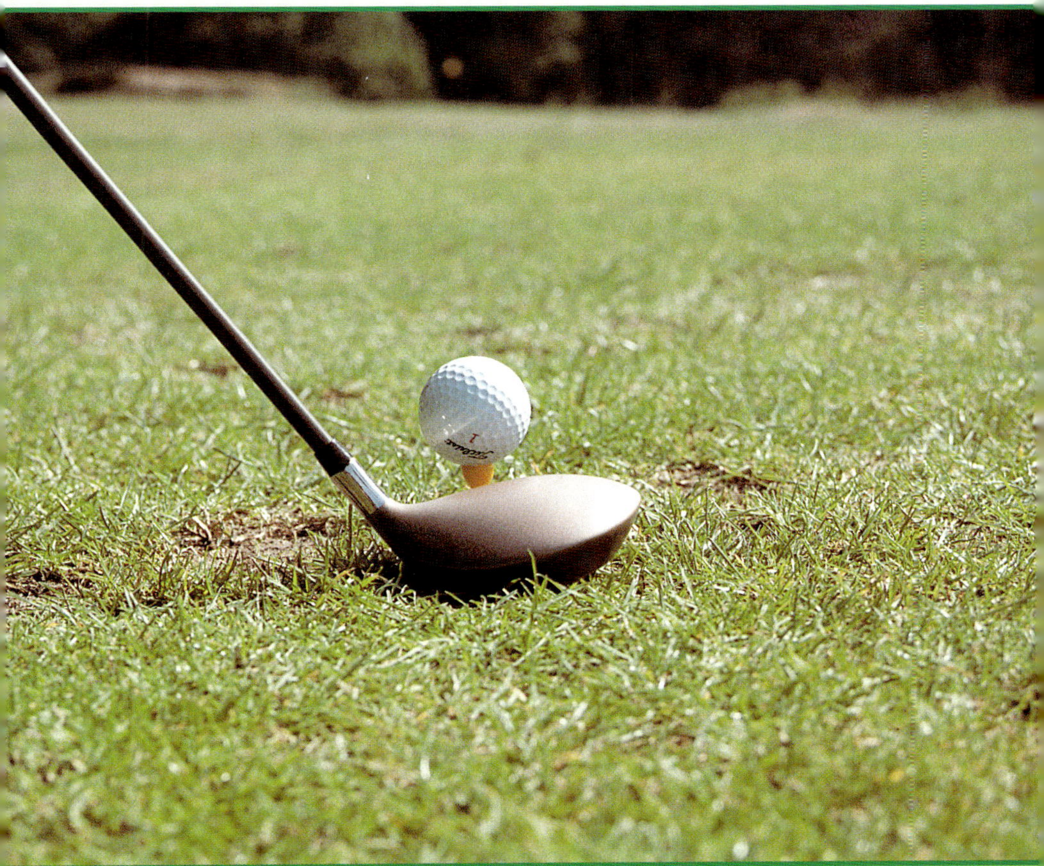

TOEING

Toeing is the term used for when the ball is hit off the toe end of the club. Although you may well feel the grip turning in your hand, the problem is most likely to be with the swing, not the grip.

Likely Causes

1. Standing too far away from the ball.

2. The ball is positioned too far forward in the stance.

3. Weight distribution is wrong with the body supported by the back of the heels.

4. The swing itself has gone wrong with the club head swinging from too far to the right of the ball to too far to the left at impact.

Cures

1. When preparing for the stroke make sure you feel comfortable with the position of the ball and the angle of the club shaft. If you still feel the ball is too far away it may be that the clubs you are using are too long for you.

2. Make sure that your weight is evenly distributed.

3. Focus on the backswing. If you have started the backswing outside the line of the ball you will hit the ball on its left side on impact. Make sure your swing goes in a much narrower arc from right to left.

57

TOPPING

A topped shot is a tee or fairway shot that struggles along the ground. A common problem for beginners, it is annoying as the longer your ball stays airborne the further it will travel. If you top your tee shot you will be struggling to make par.

Likely Causes
1. Poor weight transfer.

2. The left arm falls away during the swing, shortening the distance between you and the ball.

3. The head has been lifted during the swing.

Cures
1. Make sure that your weight shifts to your right side during the backswing and back to the left on the downswing.

2. Focus on your posture. If you find your knees or back straighten during the backswing, this is likely to be the underlying cause of your left arm falling away.

3. It is not necessary to keep your head down but you must keep it as still as possible. While this is true for all shots, if your head is moving topping is the likely result. To keep your head level you must keep your chest moving in the follow-through.

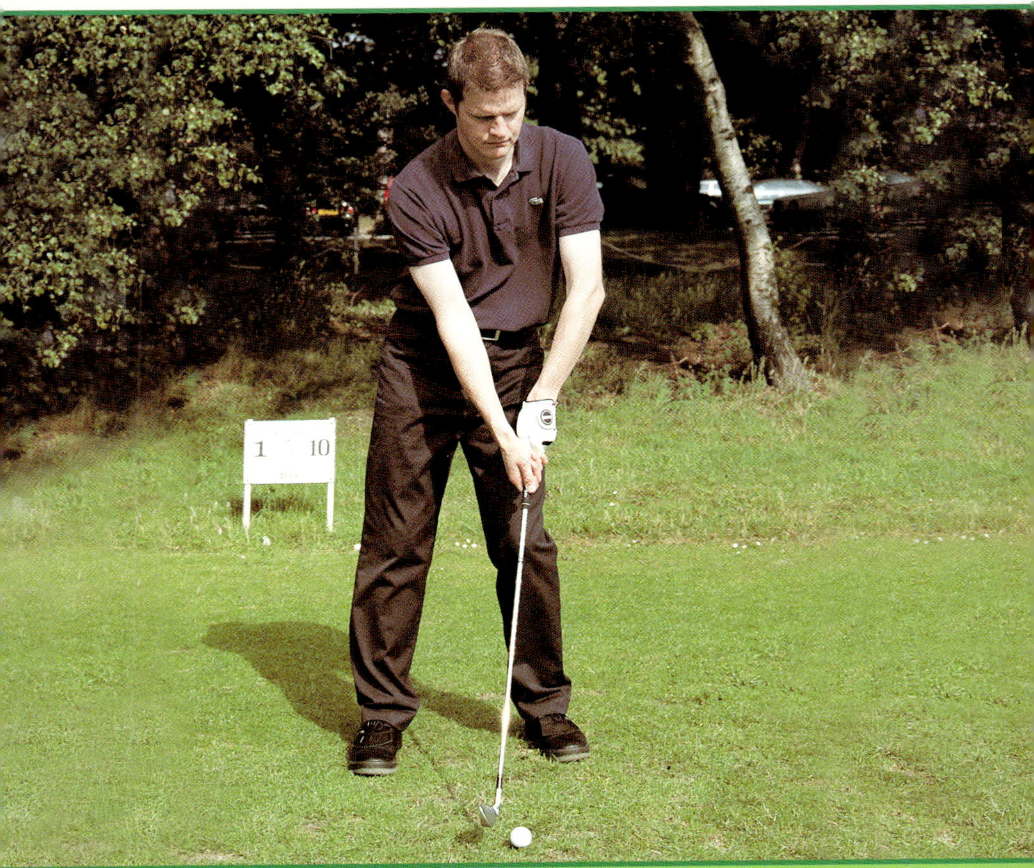
1
10

SHANKING

Shanking is the term used when the golf club strikes the ball at the point where the neck of the clubhead meets the shaft – the shank, or hosel. The ball is likely to disappear at a right angle straight into the rough. What's more, once you've started to hit shots this way, it's very difficult to stop.

Likely Causes

1. Poor weight transfer may be preventing the club face and ball meeting in the right place.

2. The arms may have moved away from the body during the downswing.

3. The swing path may be incorrect with the club coming from outside the ball to inside on impact.

Cures

1. Focus on your weight transfer and make sure that you are not moving your body towards the ball.

Also, ensure that you carry your weight on your right side, as if the weight is ahead of the ball you are in for problems.

2. Keep working on your swing until it is fluid and grooved. The arc of your swing should hit the ball dead center on impact.

61

THIN & FAT SHOTS

Thinning is a close relative of skying, and hitting the ball fat is similar to topping. With thinning, the club has connected with the topside of the ball, while hitting the ball fat means the club head has connected with the grass long before the ball. In both cases, the ball does not get off the ground.

Likely Causes of Thin Shots

1. The club connects with the ball not at the end of the downswing but in the follow-through.

2. Poor weight transfer with the weight remaining on the right side and not properly transferring to the left side as you swing.

3. In the case of tee shots it is likely that the tee peg has been set too high.

Cures

1. Revisit your swing until it has a good, fluid feel to it. Focus on weight transfer until it feels like a natural movement.

2. Push the tee lower into the ground. If you start hitting the ball well, you're in luck as it means there's nothing wrong with your swing.

Likely Causes of Fat Shots

1. The stance is too narrow, making the backswing too steep.

2. The ball has been positioned too far back in the stance.

Cures

1. Widen your stance so that the feet are level with the shoulders and you are more square-on to the ball.

2. Make sure that the ball is positioned either in the middle of your stance or almost opposite your left foot.

63

64

IMPROVING YOUR SCORE

Whether you wish to play competitively or just for fun, all players will enjoy seeing an improvement in their score. It doesn't matter how long you have been playing—there are always a few adjustments a player can make to their all-round game to improve their average score.

Firstly, add some more shots to your game, as the greater variety you have the easier it will be to adapt to the conditions on the day, and to the shot you have to play.

Then you need to add some finesse to give yourself more control and even greater accuracy. The more precise your stroke, the easier the next shot will be.

Finally, no matter what your ability, all golfers can improve their score just by staying calm and recognizing their limitations. If you are competing in a strokeplay competition, the art of not playing bad shots (easier than it sounds) will keep you in contention.

Another key is dedicated practice. Practice may be an ugly word to some but if you approach it with the right attitude, you can have fun and improve your game at the same time.

SHAPING SHOTS

The ability to both fade and draw the ball is very useful. You can get by without it but your score will come tumbling down if you can master the art of hitting the ball around a corner.

Fade
1. Make your stance wider with your shoulders pointing slightly to the left of the target.

2. Position the ball so that it is virtually opposite your left foot.

3. Open the club face and hit across the ball. The ball should travel in an arc from left to right.

Draw

1. Make your stance quite narrow with your shoulders pointing slightly to the right of the target.

2. Position the ball so that it is in the middle of your stance.

3. The arc of your swing should travel from marginally to the left of the ball to marginally to the right of the ball.

There are often opportunities on the golf course to show your creativity. If you are stuck behind a tree you may choose to play out sideways but this will cost you distance. If you can curl your ball round sharply, your ball will be that much nearer the hole for your next shot.

Apart from being behind a tree, situations where you might want to shape a shot include: being to the side of a tree and needing to keep the ball low to avoid the branches; needing to clear a water hazard or sand trap near the green but still get your ball to stop on the putting surface; and when you need to keep the ball low and out of the wind.

Deliberate Slice

There is a significant difference between a deliberate slice and an accidental one—control. When you need to hit the ball in a dramatic left-to-right arc the deliberate slice is the shot to play.

1. The ball should be positioned between the middle of your stance and your left foot.

2. Adapt your posture so that your stance is more open.

3. Although the grip remains basically the same the hands should move slightly to the left on the club. The more slice required, the further you should move your hands round.

4. Take one more club than you would normally for a shot of the same distance.

By taking these steps the club face will remain open as you cut across the ball from the outside line of the ball to the inside. This will impart spin on your ball, causing it to start left before coming back in.

Deliberate Hook

If you hook the ball naturally an error has crept into your game and you need to revisit the basics of alignment, posture and swing. Hooking the ball deliberately is different because the set-up changes and, as it is an intended shot, you will have some control of the ball's final position.

1. The ball should be positioned between the middle of your stance and your right foot.

2. Adapt your posture so that your shoulders are slightly closed.

3. The toe end of the club should be pointing inwards, by about 30 degrees.

4. Although the grip remains basically the same the hands should move slightly to the right on the club. The more hook required the further you should move your hands round.

5. Take one less club than you would normally for a shot of the same length.

By taking these actions an exaggerated in-to-out swing path will be achieved. The closed club face will make the ball roll further so you will not sacrifice too much distance.

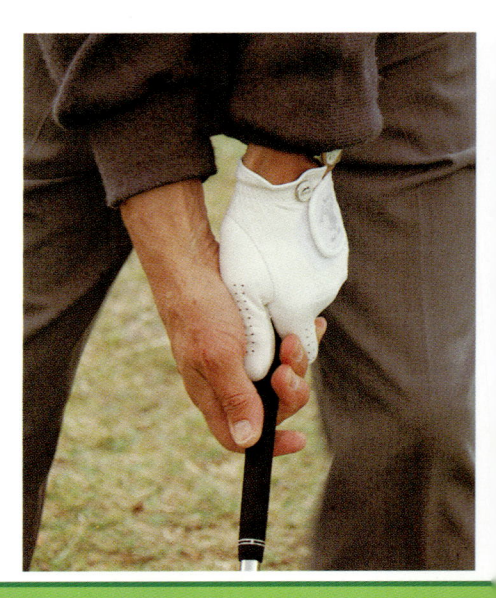

71

Lob

The well-executed lob is a very useful weapon to have in your armory as it will get you out of tight corners and help you get your ball close to the pin. Once you have mastered the shot, your main priority will be gauging distance correctly.

1. The ball should be positioned opposite your left foot.

2. Take an open stance, pointing your feet forwards at a slight angle.

3. Your shoulders and hips should point to the same degree as your feet, so that they maintain a "V" shape.

4. Your weight should be concentrated on your left side.

Your swing should then come through at a high angle, taking the club right under the ball.

Pitch and Run

The pitch and run is the shot to play on a windy day when the ball is between 50 and 150 yards from the hole. Of course, if there are sand or water traps between you and the green you'll have to give the ball some height but if it's a relatively straightforward hole it will pay you to keep the ball below the wind.

1. Adapt your posture so that your stance is relatively open.

2. The ball should be positioned between the middle of your stance and your right foot.

3. For the grip your hands should be slightly ahead of the ball.

4. Swing normally but shorten your follow-through.

GETTING BACKSPIN

All golfers would like to get backspin as they see it as a way to achieve greater accuracy. However, you need to have been playing for a while before this becomes a realistic ambition.

To get a ball to stop dead or even roll backwards on landing requires not only correct execution of the shot but also a set of conducive circumstances.

Circumstances
1. The ball needs to be lying perfectly on the fairway. Ideally the grass will be short with some give in the ground.

2. The green will need to be in good condition and be soft enough to offer the requisite grip for your ball.

The Shot
1. Club selection plays a part as you are unlikely to get backspin unless you are using a lofted club. The flatter the club face below the ball the more backspin you will achieve and so your best chance is with one of the wedges.

2. While you should set up in the same way as you would for a normal pitch shot the swing will need to be some 20-30 per cent faster as backspin requires greater club head speed. But if by swinging faster you are losing control, it is not worth your while to strive for backspin.

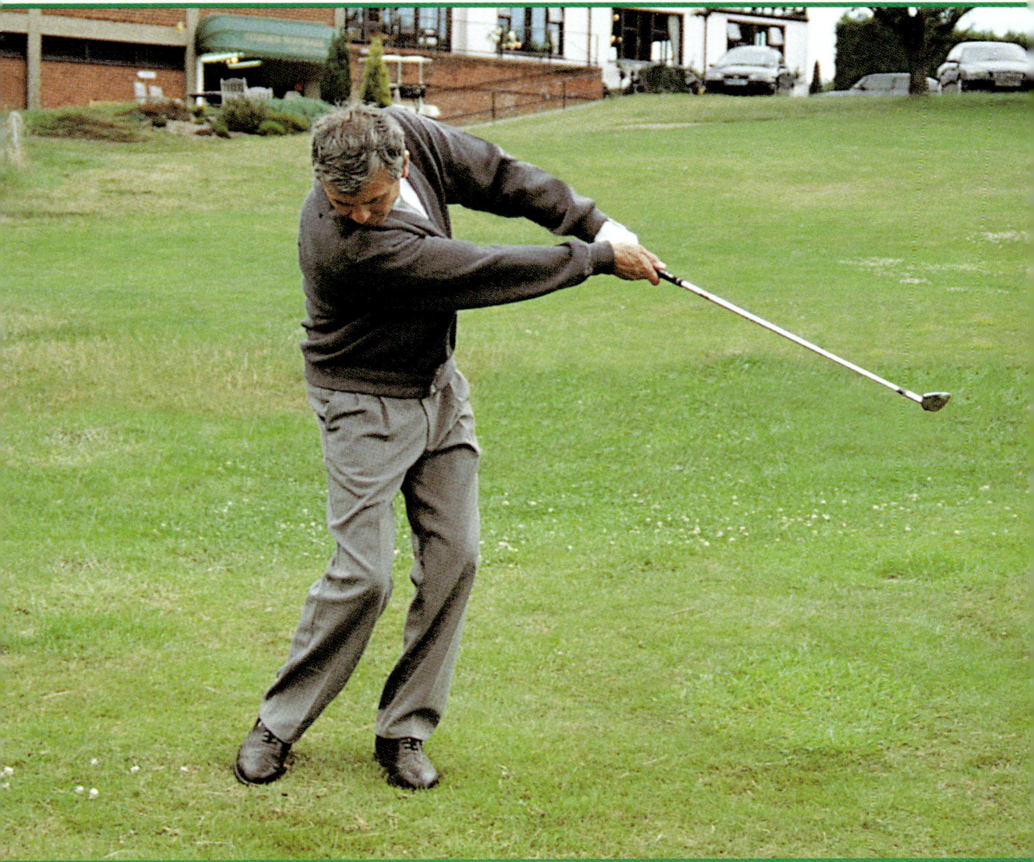

ADAPTING TO CONDITIONS

We would all like to play golf with the sun on our backs with a cooling breeze drifting across the sky. But it doesn't always work out that way and sometimes you find yourself playing in the wind and rain. The first thing to do in this situation is not to worry about the weather affecting the game but to accept and enjoy the challenge.

Playing in the Rain
1. The rain will make the course wet and soft underfoot. The softness of the ground means that the ball will not roll so far on landing. You should therefore think about taking a club with more loft than you normally would, so that the ball stays in the air for longer.

2. For pitching, the softness of the green should work in your favor as the ball is more likely to grip the surface.

3. For putting, the rain is likely to have slowed the green and you will therefore need to add a little weight to your putting.

Playing in the Wind
1. If the wind is going across or is against you, then you should aim to keep the ball low as this will limit the wind's influence on your ball's trajectory. Use a club with less loft and adapt your action as in Pitch and Run (page 73).

2. If the wind is behind, take advantage by hitting a more lofted club. Get the ball high into the air and watch as the wind obligingly pushes your ball further up the fairway.

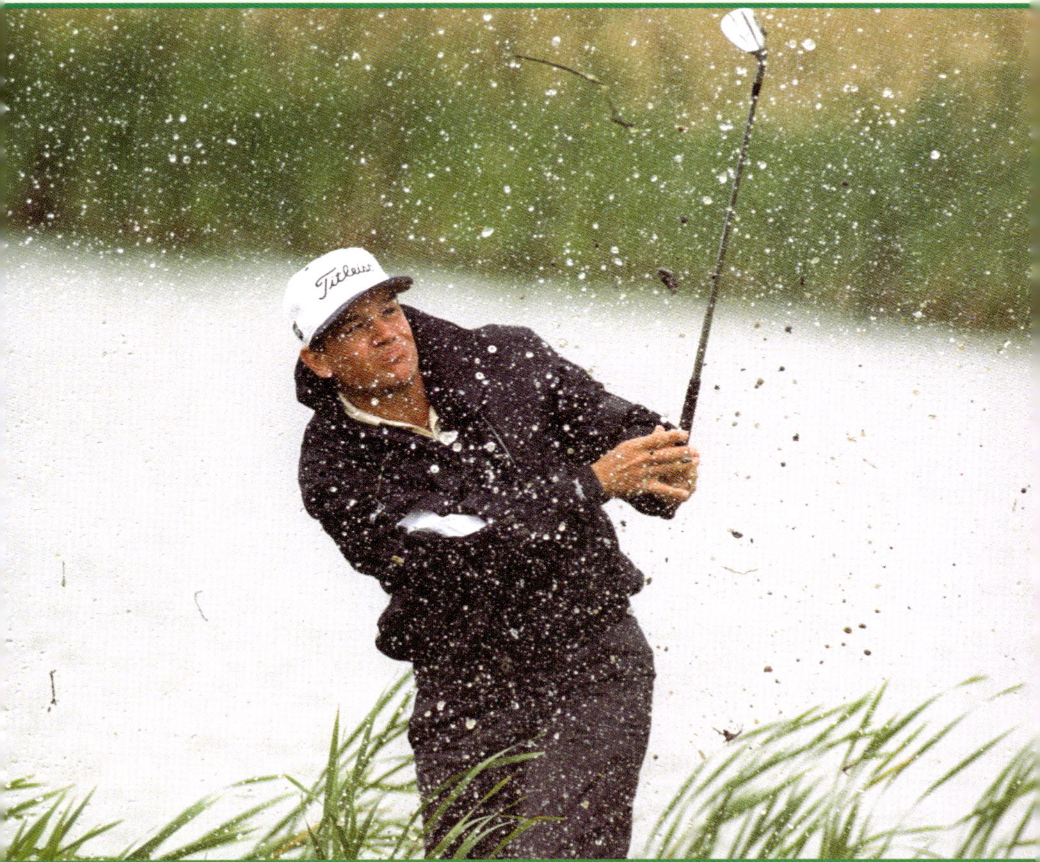
Titleist

SETTING GOALS

The ultimate goal of any golfer is to go round in par or better. To do this, your tee shots at par-4 and par-5 holes need to hit the fairway and at par-3s they need to hit the green. You must also take no more than two putts at every hole. But this won't happen unless you have been playing for a long time and on a regular basis. To know which goals you need to set, you first need a detailed analysis of your game.

1. Break down your previous five scores into drives, pitches, shots from the rough, shots from the sand trrap and putts. For drives calculate how many hit the fairway, how many went right and how many went left. For pitching, count how many hit the green. For putting, work out how many times you took more than two putts to hole out and how many you missed from under six feet.

2. Study the data this has produced and recognize the weaknesses in your game. This may sound obvious but many players will avoid the problem by trying to compensate in other areas. For example, a player who is poor off the tee but has a good short game may think that they do not need to worry about their hook or slice as they will make up the lost shot nearer the hole. The problem here is that they are putting more pressure on their short game which may then crumble.

3. Analyze the weaknesses and break them down into their components. If your problems are off the tee it may be due to your posture, alignment, grip, the swing itself, or a combination of all four. Focus on each element one at a time. Then, when you put it all together the swing should be correct.

4. Study the data again and recognize where you could improve your score just by playing more conservatively. Think about the times when you were over ambitious and played a shot at the limit of your ability that didn't come off. If you can just put the ball in the rough one less time or keep it out of the sand traps, you are sure to improve your score by at least a couple of strokes.

But the key to setting goals is to make them realistic. You should not try to improve every aspect of your game at once. Focus on one area and do not move on until you feel confident that the problem is solved. For each five times you play, aim to bring your average score down a little, rather than going for a target you are unlikely to achieve.

FITNESS & WARMING UP

Although golf makes much fewer demands than many other sports on your fitness, being in good shape will benefit your game.

The more muscular your physique, the further you will be able to hit the ball. The better your stamina the better you will be able to concentrate and thus hit consistently good shots. Of course, if you are in poor shape, it will be that much harder for you to adopt the correct posture.

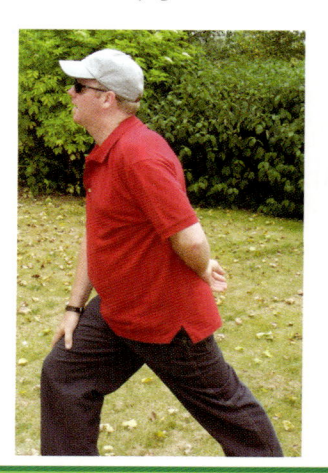

If you are not in good shape and want to improve your fitness then you should consult with your doctor or a fitness trainer before you start. They will be able to give you a routine suited to your body and your fitness levels. A few gentle exercises before you begin a round will help loosen up your body and help you to hit the ball more freely.

Warming Up

Do each of the exercises below a minimum of three times before you move on to the next one.

1. Stretch your arms and legs.

2. Keeping your chin up, turn your head from side to side.

3. Touch your toes, or as near as you can get to them.

4. With your arms above your head, lean to the left and then to the right.

5. Keeping your shoulders straight, turn your chest from left to right.

PRACTICING YOUR LONG GAME

To get full value from practice you should consider taking lessons from a professional coach. But practicing at the driving range is still worthwhile.

If you are going to practice on your own you need to be disciplined. It's all too easy to go down to the driving range with good intentions and then start hitting balls aimlessly. But if you take it seriously, the range offers the opportunity to iron out your faults and groove your shots.

If you really want to improve your game then you are going to have to put in the time. Always spend 30 minutes on the driving range before you start a round and try to have at least one additional session on the range every week.

Routine

1. Do some warm-up exercises before you start.

2. Approach each shot on the driving range as you would on the course. Focus on your grip, posture and alignment and take practice swings. There is no time pressure on the driving range and so it provides an excellent opportunity for you to groove your game. The more time you spend focusing on these elements the more a matter of routine it will become and you will find it easier to assume the correct position on the course.

3. Visualize the shot you want to play. Even though there is no pressure to be accurate on the driving range, pick out a marker in the distance and aim to get as close to it as you can.

4. Start by hitting five shots with your 5-iron. If you feel you are striking the ball well then hit five shots with your 4-iron. If not, keep hitting your 5-iron until it feels comfortable. Go through the clubs from 5-iron down until you are hitting your driver. As you will hit the ball different distances with different clubs pick out a different marker for each club you use.

5. If you hit a bad shot, don't just put down another ball and hit it. Think about where you might have gone wrong and concentrate on ironing out the fault with your next shot.

Although this is a good basic routine it would be a mistake to follow it too rigidly. Unless you are very dedicated you need to add variety to your practice or you will soon lose interest. One way to do this is to practice a different set of shots each time you're on the range. Work on your fade one day and your draw the next.

You should also consider that the driving range will not accurately reproduce the conditions on the course. If you're playing in the fall or winter, it is likely that it will be windy out on the course, so it will make sense to work on keeping the ball low.

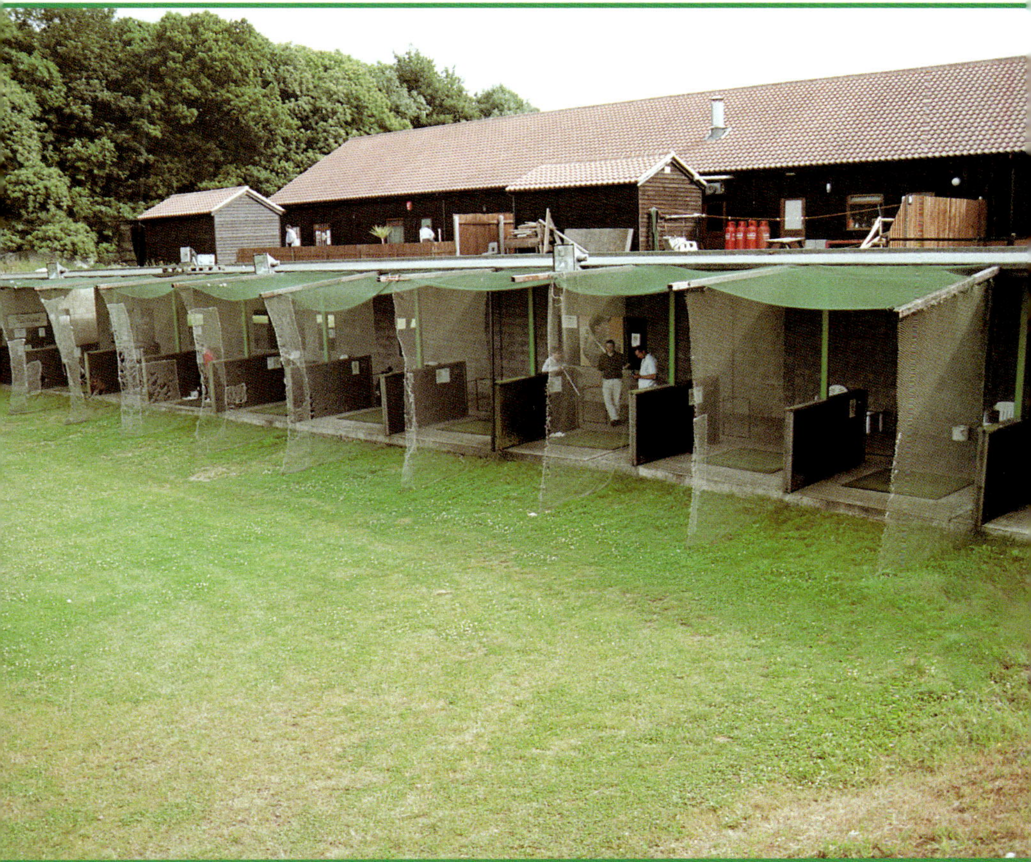

PRACTICING YOUR SHORT GAME

A successful short game requires a great variety of shots because the green will often be guarded, most probably by water hazards and sand traps. It is also likely that the pin will have been positioned in an awkward spot.

For example, your ball may have stopped just short of a greenside sand trap and the pin may be just on the other side of the sand. The challenge will be to loft the ball over the sand trap and get it to stop as soon as it lands. As with the long game, ideally you should practice at least once a week.

Pitching and Chipping Routine

1. Do some warm-up exercises before you start.

2. Visualize the shot you intend to play. The nearer you are to the hole the greater accuracy you require. While beginners should start with the aim of simply getting the ball onto the green, as you become more experienced you should try to get the ball as near to the pin as possible.

3. As with practicing your long game you should approach each shot as you would on the course. Focus on your grip, posture and alignment and take practice swings before each shot.

4. Begin by placing balls 70 yards from the green. Practice from different lies and with different clubs. This will help you to develop feel, a crucial element for a successful short game. Keep going until you have got five balls on the green.

5. Move up to 60 yards from the green and go through the same routine. Keep moving ten yards forward and complete the routine when you have put five balls on the green from twenty yards. The nearer you are to the green the nearer you should try to get your ball to the flag.

If your garden is big enough you can practice at home by putting a bucket down on the grass and, taking fifty balls, see what percentage you can get into the bucket. Go through the exercise as often as you can and try to improve your percentage each time. It may seem like a stiff challenge, but as long as you don't lose confidence in your ability you should be rewarded on the course.

Sand Trap Routine

1. As per usual, do some warm-up exercises before you start and go through your pre-shot routine before each stroke.

2. Start with a relatively easy shot from the middle of the sand trap. When you have successfully executed it five times move your ball slightly nearer the lip of the bunker so that the angle is steeper. Go through the same routine, and stop when the ball is two feet from the lip.

3. Go through the same routine as above, but this time moving the ball from the middle to the back of the sand trap.

4. Again, go through the same routine, but this time moving the ball to the side of the sand trap.

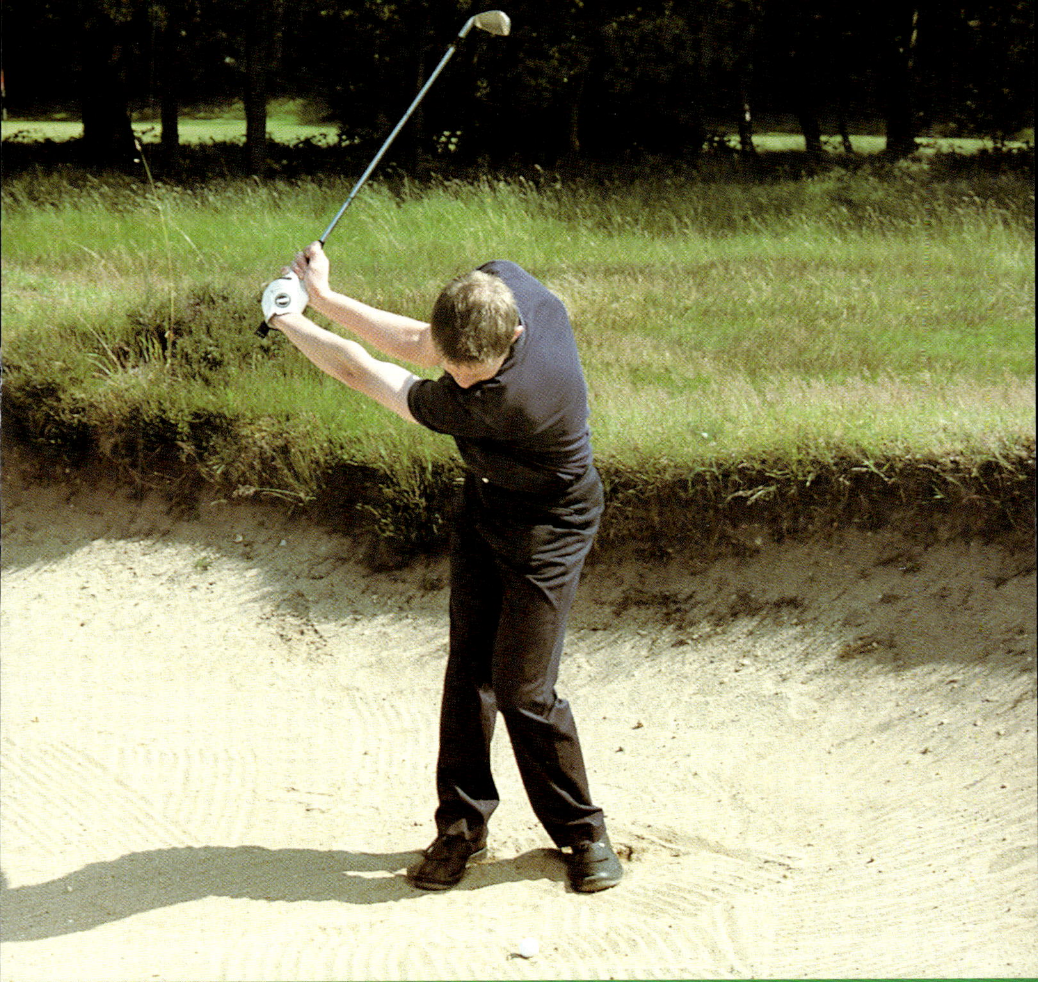

PRACTICING YOUR PUTTING

Improving your putting will make a major difference to your score. The par for each hole is calculated to include two putts which means you are expected to take 36 putts each time you play. That means that on a typical golf course half your shots will be putts if you are to go round in level par.

Putting is largely a matter of feel and this can only be achieved by many hours of practice. You should remember that a different grip is required and also that your swing should be the same as for other shots, albeit with a shorter backswing and follow-through.

It is definitely worth your while to spend some time on the practice putting surface just before you play a round as this will help you to get a feel for the speed of the greens on the day.

Routine

1. Begin by placing your ball five feet from the hole. It is incredibly frustrating to miss from this distance on the course so you should be aiming to sink every one. Keep practicing from this distance until you have got ten in the hole in succession. If you are having problems you should check that your dominant eye is over the ball, that the swing is smooth and that you are hitting the ball off the middle of the club face.

2. Move the ball back to ten feet from the hole. You should hope to get a high percentage in from this distance so keep going until you have got seven out of ten to drop. As you get further back from the hole reading the green will become more important.

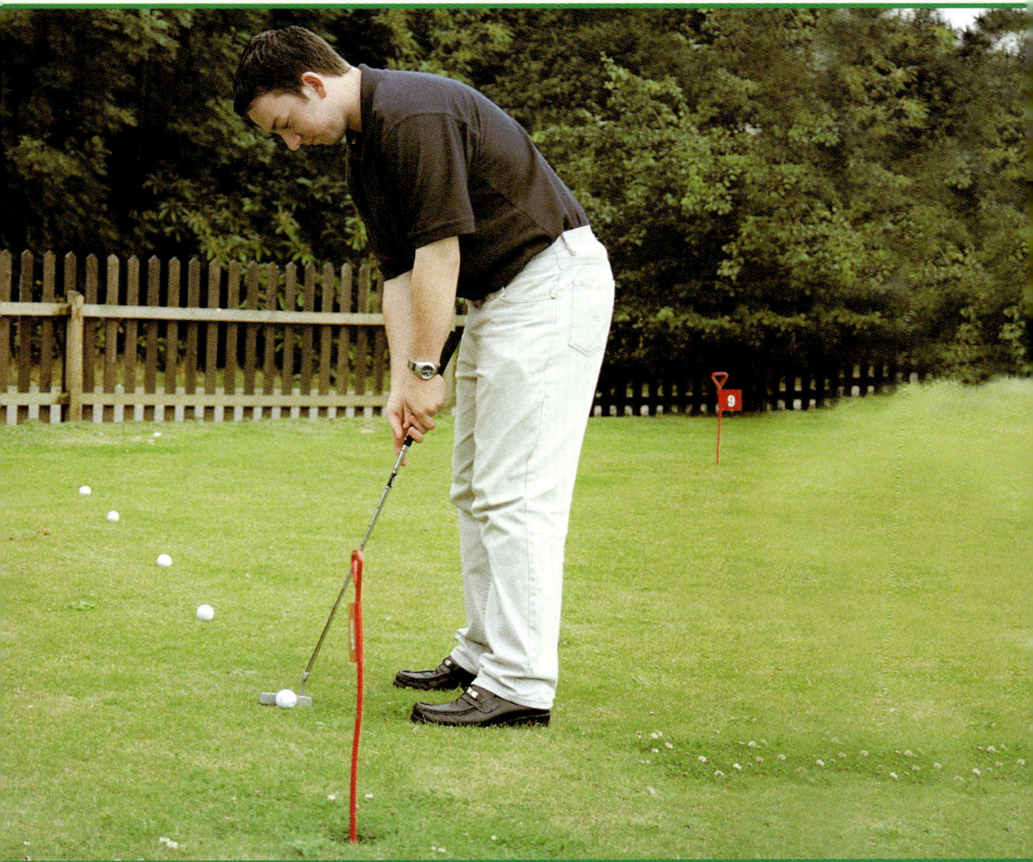
9

You should kneel behind your ball and look at the ground, carefully searching for contours that will affect your ball's journey.

3. Move the ball back to fifteen feet from the home and aim to hole five of the ten.

4. Keep moving the ball back in increments of five. From 20, 25 and 30 feet your aim should be to make sure you take no more than two putts to sink your ball.

Vary this routine by moving to a different angle from the hole for each distance. This should give you the opportunity to play shots from above and below the hole. By practicing strokes which require a different weight of shot you will add feel to your game.

93

MENTAL STRENGTH

There are so many elements to your game that could go wrong that it is easy to succumb to nerves. It's all too easy to arrive at the first tee worried that you are going to make a fool of yourself by shanking your first shot.

Before You Play

One obvious way to deal with these nerves is to give yourself a pre-round routine. If you arrive at the course five minutes before your tee time you are just making trouble for yourself. Aim to arrive 45 minutes before you are due on the course and head for the driving range. Spend a good twenty minutes there loosening up your muscles and hitting shots. Then go to the practice putting surface and hole a few putts. As you have now hit a few good shots you should be confident of doing so from the first tee.

On the Course

On the course you should never let a bad shot play on your mind. There's nothing you can do about it once you've hit it so you need to forget about it and concentrate on the next shot. Similarly, if your playing partner is longer off the tee than you are don't try to keep up or outhit them, as you will only succeed in losing control of your own shot. You are much more likely to beat your opponent by concentrating on making the most of your own game.

No matter what your standard, you can improve your score by managing the course sensibly. Your plan should be to get from tee to green as safely as possible. Remember that the most direct route may not be the best option.

Generally, try and adhere to a consistent method on your swing during a round, and leave more major adjustment to the driving range.

95

COURSE MANAGEMENT

From the Tee
Imagine there are trees on the left of a narrow fairway and sand traps 180 yards up on the right. The green is a further 100 yards away on the left-hand side. You naturally hit the ball 170 yards with your 3-iron. By aiming left you run the risk of going into the trees, by aiming right you might get caught in the sand trap.

In this situation many players will take a big swing and try and clear the sand traps. They might get away with it but it is more likely that they will either hook the ball into the trees or land in the sand trap. The sensible option is to take a 5-iron, and knock it 150 yards up the right. You have taken the trees on the left out of play and haven't taken a chance with the sand trap. You still have a shot to the green and with a right-to-left angle you have more of the green to play with.

From the Fairway
For fairway shots you should apply the same principles as you would for tee shots. Never go for shots which you only have a ten per cent chance of making. It is always much better to stay in control by laying up short than to attempt to smash the ball as far as you can.

It is much harder to play shots out of the rough or sand traps, so simply by staying out of them you will improve your score. When aiming for the green concentrate on getting the ball on the putting surface rather than near the hole.

From Around the Green
If you have missed the green you should try to leave yourself with an uphill putt from your chip. These are much easier to control than downhill putts which can continue to roll long after they have missed the hole.

On the Green

No matter where you are on the green you should aim to take no more than two putting strokes. If you are a long way away imagine that the hole is six feet wide and aim to get your ball into this circle. This way the target you are giving yourself is virtually unmissable. As you should be holing six-foot putts nine times out of ten this should see you taking no more than two putts nearly every time.

For shorter putts you should never leave your ball short of the hole. It is very frustrating to realize that your ball never had a chance of dropping into the hole because there was not enough weight to your shot. As long as the green is not too fast, and your putt is straight, you should aim for a spot two feet beyond the hole. If the putt is on the right line the ball will still be traveling slowly enough to drop.

Getting it to the Green

As the illustrations show, there are no hard and fast ways to play a hole.

The solid lines show good percentage play, whereas the dotted lines show the riskier routes to the pin.

99

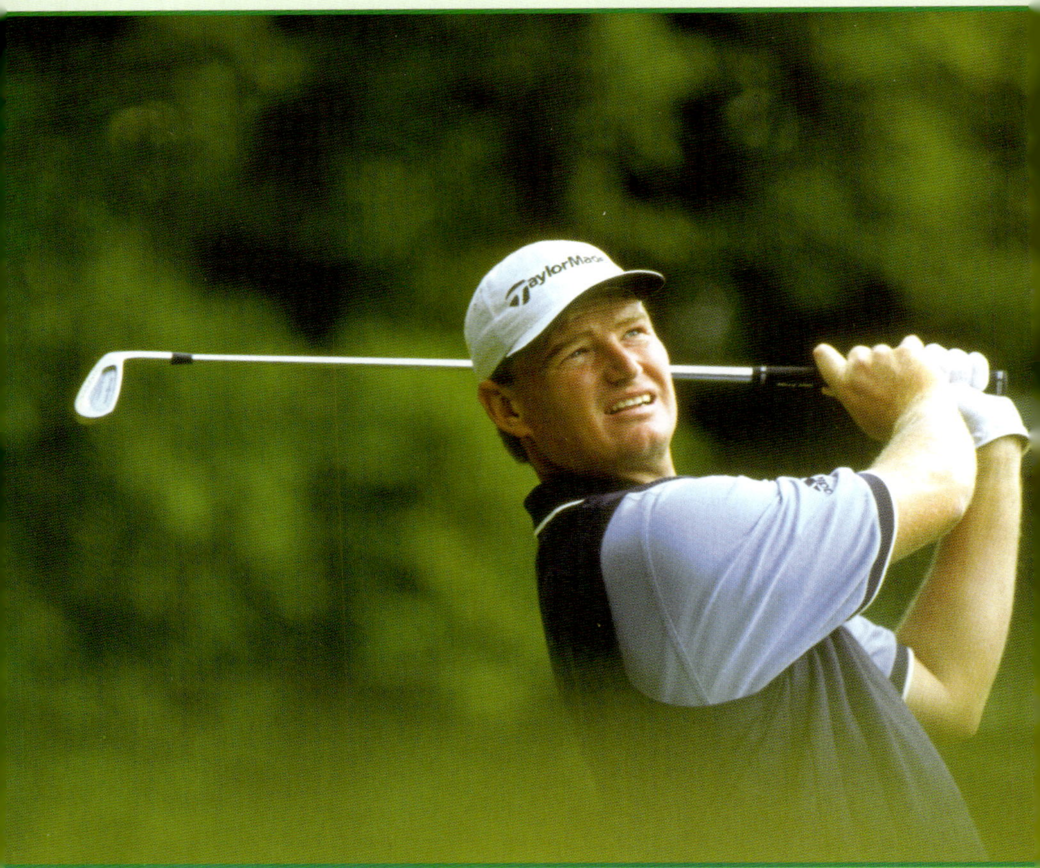
TaylorMade

ON THE COURSE

When you've got the golf bug it's only natural to want to find out more about the game and this section is a good place to start.

You'll find out how to get a handicap and the types of competition you can play, you'll get a taste of the game's etiquette and rules and you can find out about the great tournaments and their champions.

To the outsider the etiquette to be observed on the course may seem like an unnecessary nuisance but it is part of the game's mystique and appeal. When the beginner knows the conventions of the game's etiquette he or she will find it a pleasure to be surrounded by people who are unfailingly polite and will soon find themselves behaving in the same way.

If the chance arises, take the opportunity to watch a professional tournament. You will be stunned to see how far the professionals can hit the ball and what shots they can conjure up, despite the pressure of having a large audience in attendance.

THE HANDICAP SYSTEM

The handicap system enables players of different abilities to play alongside each other in friendly or competitive games.

In basic terms a player's handicap is the number of strokes a player may deduct from their actual score to adjust their scoring ability to the level of a non-handicapped golfer. It is designed to allow golfers of different abilities to compete on the same level. Working out your handicap may seem difficult at first but ask your club to assist you in calculating it, or try using one of the many online calculators.

A player's course handicap is determined by multiplying their USGA handicap index by the USGA slope rating of the course played and then dividing by 113. The resulting figure is rounded off to the nearest whole number. Alternatively, or when in competition, a player can check their handicap index against the handicap conversion chart for the tee marker from which they will play. These charts are available at all member clubs. Once a playing handicap is determined, it is then used to produce a net score for the competition.

To discover a player's handicap index the average of their best handicap differentials (the percentage of scores used in a scoring record decreases from the maximum of the best 50 per cent as the number of scores in the scoring record decreases) is multiplied by 0.96, numbers after tenths are ignored. A player's handicap differential can be worked out using the following formula:

Handicap differential = (adjusted gross score − USGA course rating) x 113/ USGA slope rating

Slope rating

A course's slope rating can be used as an indicator as to its difficulty; the higher the number, the tougher the course. Slope is based on a USGA formula that incorporates 10 different factors including length and number of hazards. Nationally, the slope rating of an average course is about 113.

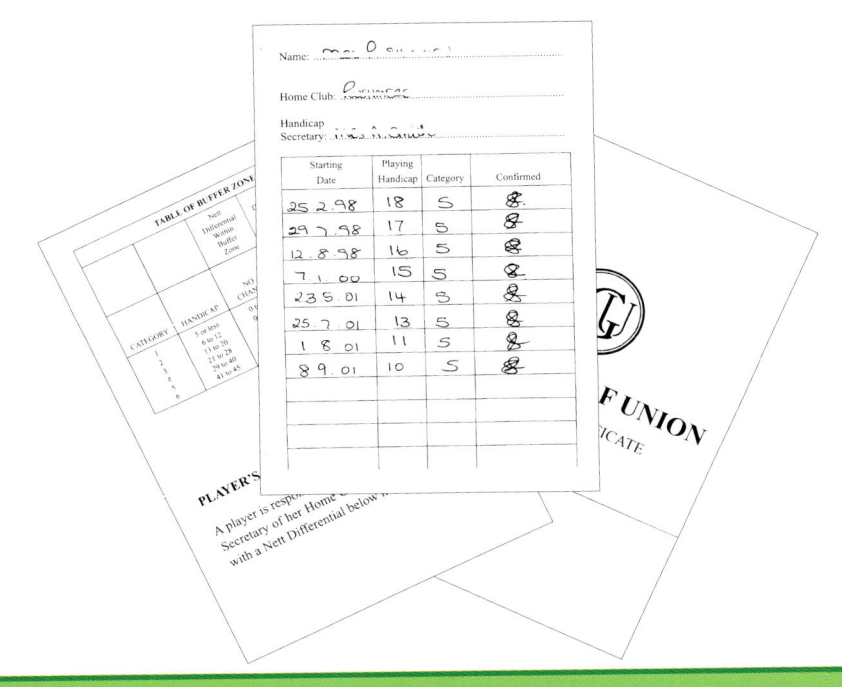

TYPES OF COMPETITION

Typically, you and your partners will play against each other either using the strokeplay or matchplay system.

In strokeplay the winner is the player who takes the fewest strokes and in matchplay the winner is the player who wins the most holes. Officially recognized competitions will usually either be between two players, or teams of two.

Fourball

A fourball can be played as either a matchplay or strokeplay competition. Played by two teams of two, each player plays his own ball. However, only the best individual score for each side for each hole is recorded.

Foursome

Played by two teams of two, each side plays one ball, the partners playing alternate shots.

Texas Scramble

There are many variants to the Texas Scramble but in general it is played by teams of four. Each player tees off and then three balls are picked up and each player then plays another shot from the position of the best tee shot. This continues until the ball is in the hole. As with the fourball and foursome the Texas Scramble can be played as either a matchplay or strokeplay competition.

Stableford

Only suitable for strokeplay, Stablefords can be played by teams of between one and four. While each player plays a normal round the Stableford offers a different way of scoring. The scoring system for each hole is 2 or more over par: 0 points, 1 over par: 1 point, par: 2 points, 1 under par: 3 points, 2 under par: 4 points, 3 under par: 5 points. The score for each hole is then added up —the highest total score wins.

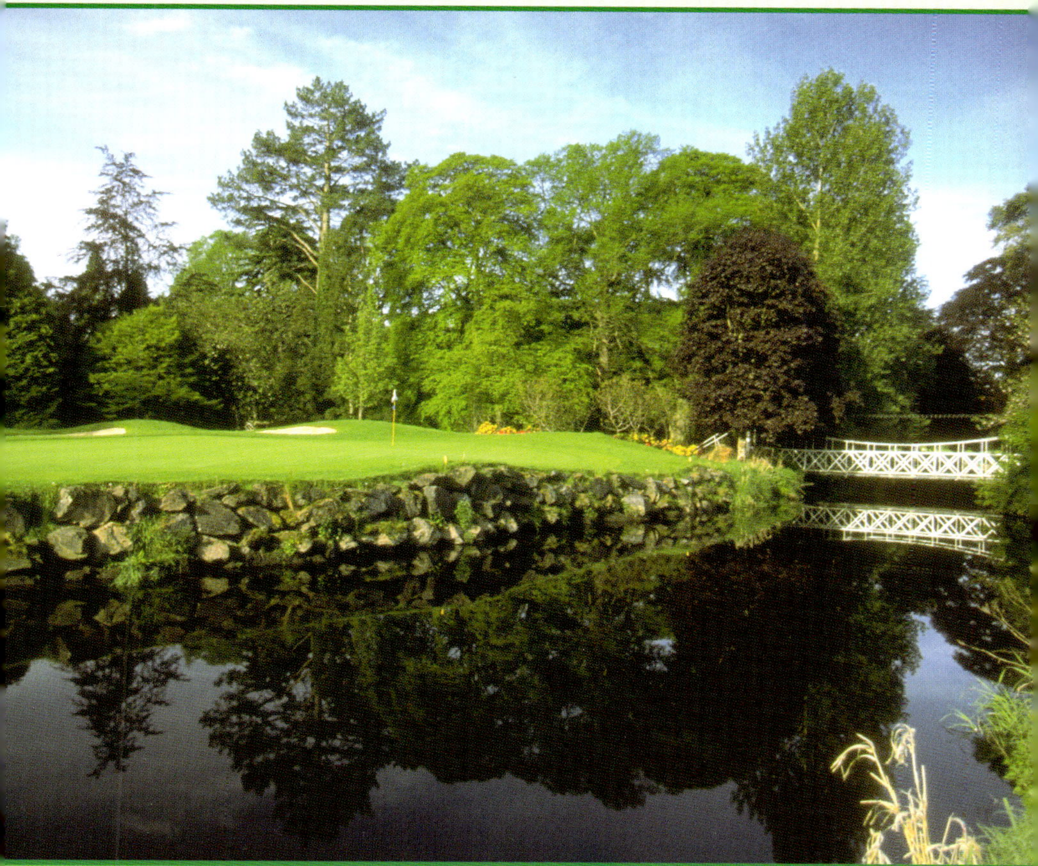

RULES OF GOLF

The official rules of golf are issued in a book by the Royal and Ancient Golf Club of St Andrews which is well worth having. This covers the rules in all the detail you are likely to need but below we have listed just some of the more important ones. You should also bear in mind that all clubs have local rules which should also be respectfully obeyed.

The total number of clubs in your bag should never exceed fourteen. But if you start with fewer, you can add other clubs during the round, so long as the total never exceeds fourteen.

Declaring a false handicap will result in disqualification from competition.

When teeing off, the tee peg should be laid between or behind the two markers. You cannot lay it ahead of the markers.

You can only use a tee peg for tee shots.

If your tee shot goes out of bounds or is lost then you incur a penalty stroke and you must play another tee shot. The second tee shot will therefore be your third stroke. If you are not sure if your ball can be played then you can hit a provisional tee shot. Again this will be your third stroke but if your original ball is found in a playable position then you must continue playing with that one.

If your ball is headed out of bounds but then strikes an obstacle and comes back into play that is your good luck. It is only where the ball finishes that matters.

If you lose your ball or go out of bounds with a shot other than a tee shot the penalty is one stroke. You should drop your ball as near to the spot where it was last seen or if the ball went out of bounds, within one club's length of the out-of-bounds markers.

You may only look for a lost ball for five minutes.

In general, you cannot improve the lie of your ball. There are exceptions to this rule and you should consult your local club if you are in doubt.

If you are in a sand trap you are not allowed to touch the ground with your club before you play the stroke, nor remove any impediments in the sand trap, nor smooth the sand. However, you may move impediments on the green with your hand or club.

You cannot play the ball while it is moving.

If you miss the ball completely—an airshot—it counts as a stroke and you must add one to your total.

If when you are putting you hit the flagstick it is a two-stroke penalty. You should therefore make sure it has been taken out of the hole before your ball reaches it.

If your ball lands in casual water (for example a puddle caused by heavy rain, not a water hazard) or ground under repair you may move it to another spot. To ensure you get no advantage, you must 'drop' the ball no nearer the hole.

To drop the ball, you must stand up straight, hold the ball at shoulder height with your arm fully extended and then let go. If it rolls back into the casual water or ground under repair you must drop it again.

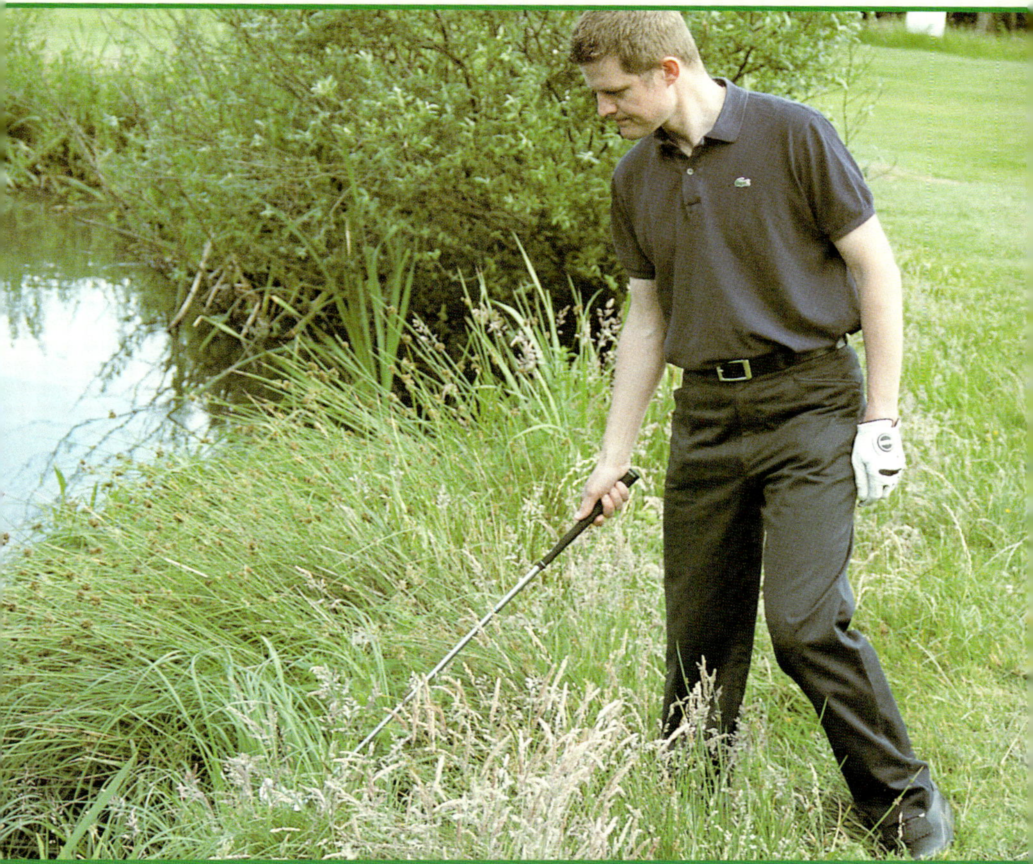

MEMBERS
ONLY

ETIQUETTE

The importance of etiquette on the golf course is often exaggerated by those who wish to mock the game. In reality, however, much of what is described as etiquette is really a mixture of simple good manners and common sense.

The Don'ts

Don't play a stroke or a practice swing if there is a danger of hitting someone with your club.

Don't stand in the eyeline of a golfer about to play a stroke.

Don't hold up play. If the group behind are catching you up let them "play through."

Don't play your tee or fairway shot if you can reach the group ahead of you. It is for that group to let you through, not for you to bully them.

Don't touch the ground with your practice swings on the tee. If you find it necessary to touch the ground, then take your practice swings away from the tee.

Don't make any attempt to put your partner off.

Don't put your golf bag on the green or tee and always obey the local rules regarding where you can take your trolley.

Don't walk across the line of another player's shot on the green.

Don't mark your scorecard on the green as this will hold up players behind. Either do it on your way to the next tee or at the next tee.

The Do's

Do stand behind and to the right of the golfer playing their tee shot. You will not put them off and you will not be hit by a stray shot.

Do shout "Fore!" if you are worried your ball is going to hit someone. A golf ball has the potential to cause a great deal of injury so you should also apologize profusely for being so foolish as to hit your ball when there was a chance it might hurt someone.

Do repair divots on the fairway and pitch marks on the green and do rake the sand trap after you have played your shot. It is not fair on players behind you if you do not repair damage you have made. Even if players ahead of you have not repaired their damage that does not excuse you of your responsibilities.

Do allow the player who has won the previous hole "the honor" of playing the first stroke at the next hole.

Do congratulate your opponents when they play good shots.

Do acknowledge other groups of players you may come across on the course.

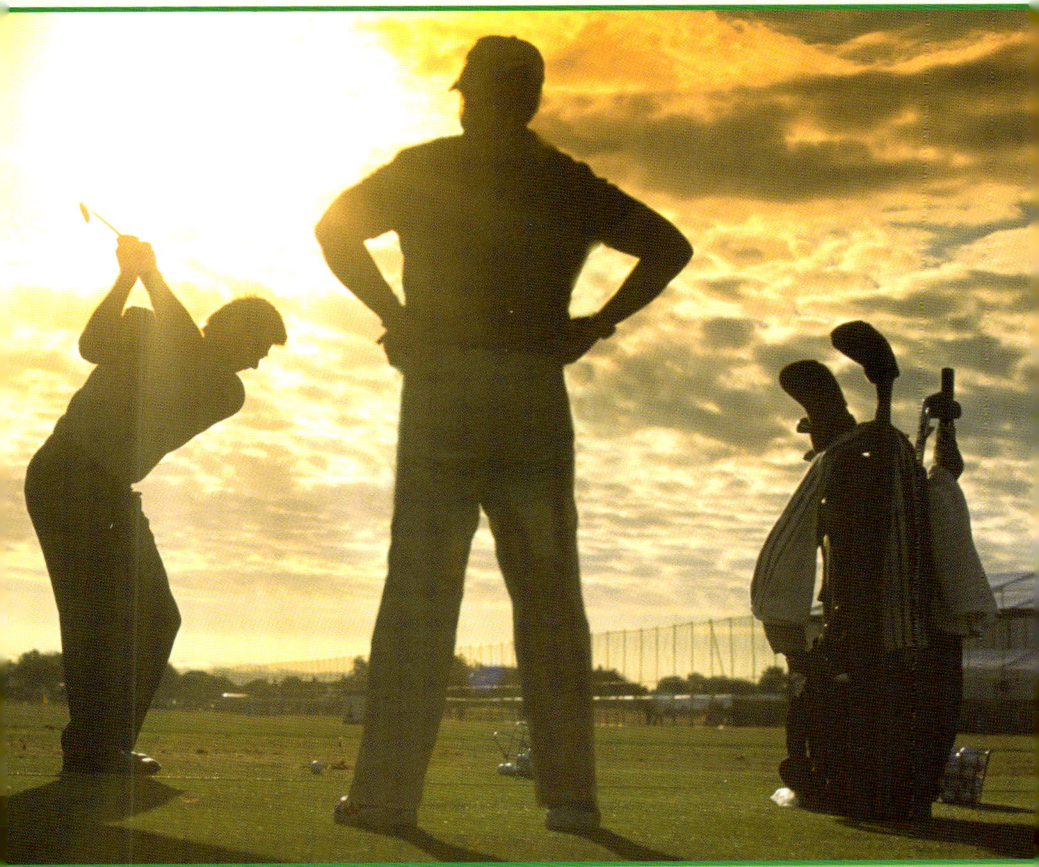

RECORDS

First Open

Golf's first Open Championship took place in Scotland in 1860. It was won by Willie Park Sr, who went on to win it again 1863, 1866 and 1875.

Most Majors

With eighteen triumphs Jack Nicklaus holds the record for the most wins in the majors: the British Open (three), the US Open (four), the US Masters (six) and the US PGA (five). He stands alone as the only player to record six wins at the US Masters.

All-time Money Man

Eldrick "Tiger" Woods holds the record for all-time career earnings on the US PGA circuit. Between August 1996 and March 2001 he earned $23,767,307. Of that amount, $9,188,321 was earned in the 2000 season alone, another world record. In 1997, aged just 21, he became the youngest-ever winner of the US Masters.

Ryder Cup Records
Englishman Nick Faldo (below) holds the record for the most individual wins in this team competition with 23 wins from 46 matches. The best record on the American side is held by Arnold Palmer with 22 wins.

Golf in Space
Golf became the first sport to be played in space when American astronaut Alan Shepard hit a couple of shots with a 6-iron on the moon in 1971.

Solheim Cup Star
The record for most individual wins in the Solheim Cup team competition is held by American Dottie Pepper. Up to 2002 she had won thirteen matches.

Most British Open Wins
Jersey-born Harry Vardon has won more British Open titles than any other player. He won his six titles between 1896 and 1914.

Most US Open Wins
The record for most US Open wins (four) is held by four different players: Willie Anderson, Bobby Jones Jr, Ben Hogan and Jack Nicklaus.

Most US PGA Wins
The record for most wins of the US PGA tournament is shared by Walter Hagen (below) and Jack Nicklaus, who have both recorded five victories.

Fast Money
In 1999 Australian Karrie Webb (below), aided by six tournament wins, became the first female golfer to win over a million dollars in a single season on the US LPGA tour.

TOURNAMENTS & CHAMPIONS

The tournaments generally recognized as the most significant in the golfing calendar are the US Masters, the British Open, the US Open and the US PGA. The main team competitions are the Ryder Cup, for men, and its female equivalent, the Solheim Cup.

The US Masters

Always held in Augusta, Florida, the US Masters was first played in 1934 when it was won by Horton Smith.

Since 1949 the closing ceremony has included the presentation of the famous green jacket to the winner by the previous year's winner.

In 1997 Tiger Woods won by twelve strokes, the biggest-ever winning margin. As he was just 21 years old at the time, he also became the youngest-ever winner.

In 1986 Jack Nicklaus became the oldest-ever winner of the tournament at the age of 46.

Only three players have won the tournament two years running: Jack Nicklaus, Tiger Woods and Nick Faldo.

The British Open

The British Open is the oldest of the four majors. The first tournament was played at Prestwick in 1860 when Willie Park Sr. won.

Since 1872 the tournament's location has moved each year.

Five-time winner Tom Watson (right) won at a different course each time. His triumphs have come at Carnoustie, Turnberry, Muirfield, Royal Birkdale and Troon.

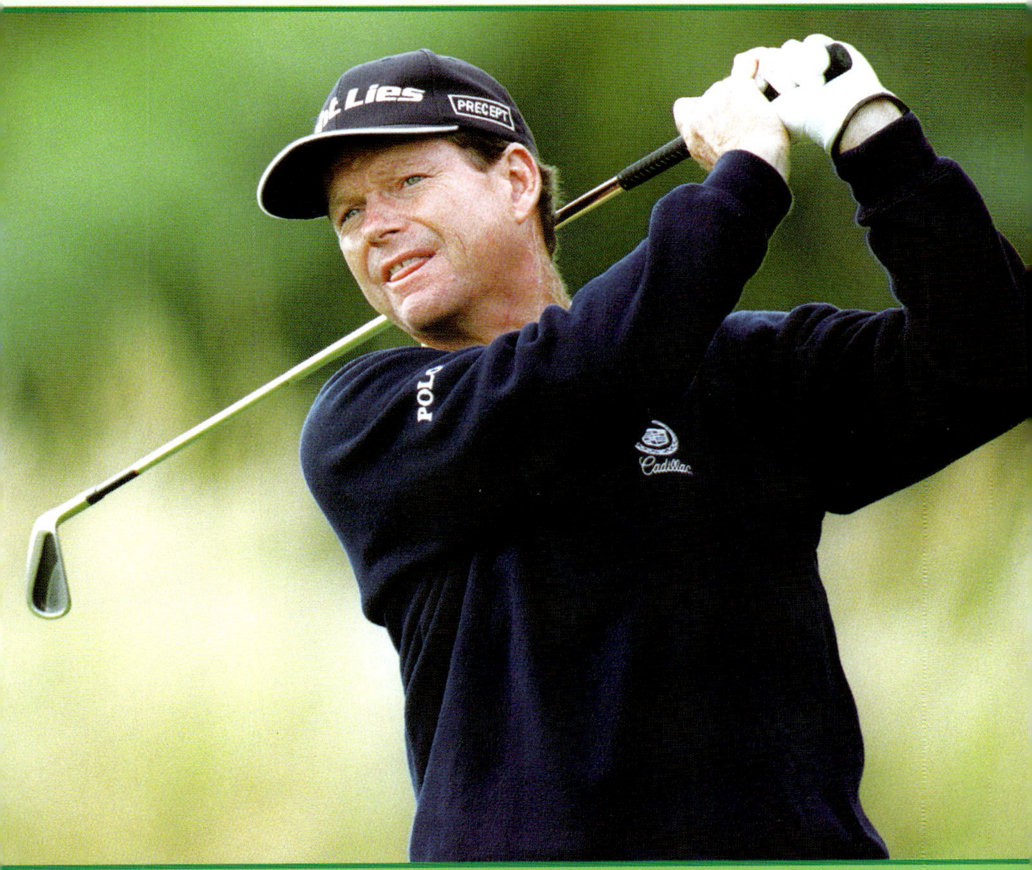
PRECEPT
POLO
Cadillac

The early years were dominated by Old Tom Morris and his son Young Tom Morris who both won the event four times. Old Tom is the oldest-ever winner (46) and Young Tom the youngest-ever winner (17).

Since the 1870s the closing ceremony has included the presentation of the famous Claret Jug to the winner.

When Scot Paul Lawrie (below) won the tournament in 1999 he was a record ten shots behind the leader at the beginning of the final round.

The US Open

The US Open, first played in 1895, is played at a number of different courses.

The oldest winner is American Hale Irwin (below) who was 45 when he triumphed in 1990.

In 2000 Tiger Woods smashed the record for biggest winning margin, leading the field home by fifteen strokes.

In 1938 Ray Ainsley took nineteen shots to complete a single hole.

The US PGA

The last of the majors to be played each season, the tournament began in 1916.

The cup awarded to the winner is known as the Wanamaker Trophy.

The oldest winner is Julius Boros, who was 48 when he won in 1968. The youngest winner is Gene Sarazen, who was 20 when he triumphed in 1922.

When Colin Montgomerie (below) lost after a play-off with Steve Elkington in 1997 he could consider himself unfortunate as they had both finished seventeen under par – a new record

The Ryder Cup

The Ryder Cup was first competed for in 1926 between America and the British Isles.

The competition proved so one-sided that after 1977 the British team became a European team.

The USA has recorded 24 wins and seven defeats. There have also been two draws.

The Solheim Cup

The women's equivalent to the Ryder Cup, the Solheim Cup has only been played for since 1990. The USA has won four times and Europe twice.

GLOSSARY

Ace .... hole in one.
Air shot .... a complete miss of the ball.
Albatross .... three under par on a single hole.
Apron .... short fringe of golf that often surrounds the green.
Attending the flag ..... holding the flag for another player and then removing it from the hole as the putted ball approaches.
Back nine .... the last nine holes of an eighteen-hole course.
Ball marker .... the object used to mark a ball's position on the green before it is picked up.
Birdie .... one under par on a single hole.
Bite .... a term used to refer to a ball which stops quickly because of backspin.
Bogey .... one over par on a single hole.
Break .... the way a putt will run due to the contours of the green.
Buggy .... powered cart which players may use to transport themselves around the course.
Bunker .... alternative name for the sand trap.
Caddie .... a person who carries the player's clubs round the course.
Carry .... the distance a ball travels in the air.
Casual water .... water on the course (e.g. puddles) which is not an official hazard. A player may get relief from casual water.

Choke	the playing of a poor shot due to nerves.
Closed face	when the club face is pointed slightly inward.
Club face	the part of the club that connects with the ball.
Club head	the part of the club that includes the club face.
Clubs	equipment used to hit the ball.
Cup	another term for the hole on the green itself.
Cut	in four-round competitions the field is cut after two rounds. The players at the back of the field are excluded from the rest of the competition.
Dimples	the indentations on a golf ball.
Divot	piece of turf lifted from the ground when a shot is played.
Dogleg	a hole that bends either to the left or right so that you cannot see part or all of the green from the tee.
Dormie	term used in matchplay competition when a team or player can no longer lose the match although a tie is still possible.
Double bogey	two over par on a single hole.
Downhill lie	when the ball you intend to hit lies on the downslope.
Draw	to move the ball in the air from right to left.
Drive	shot from the tee.
Driver	a 1-wood used for long tee shots.
Driving range	area set aside for practice.

Eagle	two under par on a single hole.
Fade	to move the ball in the air from left to right.
Fairway	the area between the tee and green, excluding hazards.
Fat	shot hitting the ground well before the ball.
Flagstick	marker for where the hole is on the green.
Flier	a ball which has traveled further than expected.
Fore!	the warning cry to use if someone is in danger of being hit by your ball.
Fourball	a competition between two teams of two, each player playing his own ball.
Foursome	a type of competition between two teams of two where partners take alternate shots.
Front nine	the first nine holes of an eighteen-hole golf course.
Get down in two	to take no more than two shots to get the ball into the hole from around the green.
Gimmie	a shot so close to the hole there is no need for your opponent to make you play.
Green	the putting surface.
Green fee	the charge made to play a particular course.
Grip	the part of the club the golfer holds and also the style in which the club is held.
Grooves	the indentations in the club face.

Gross score . . . . .the score for eighteen holes before the handicap is taken into account.
Ground under repair . . . . .a damaged area on the course from which you may receive a free drop.
Gutta percha . . . . .rubbery material used to make early golf balls.
Hacker . . . . .a golfer of limited ability.
Halve . . . . .when players take the same score for a hole or round.
Handicap . . . . .the system used to enable golfers of different ability to compete on equal terms.
Hazard . . . . .any feature on the course designed to make play more difficult.
Heel . . . . .where the club head meets the shaft.
Hole in one . . . . .when the tee shot goes in the hole.
Hole out . . . . .to play the last shot of the hole.
Honor . . . . .the player who wins the hole has the honor of playing the first shot at the next hole.
Hook . . . . .a shot that goes sharp left in the air.
Impact . . . . .when the club face strikes the ball.
Interlocking grip . . . . .a style of holding the club.
Iron . . . . .any one of the numbered iron-headed clubs.
Lie . . . . .the resting position of a ball.
Line . . . . .the trajectory of a ball.

Links	any golf course within four miles of the coast.
Lip	the edge of the hole on the green.
Local rules	rules related to a particular course.
Long game	refers to shots over 180 yards.
Majors	four important tournaments: the US Masters, British Open, US Open and US PGA.
Matchplay	form of competition where holes are won, lost or halved.
Net score	a player's score after their handicap has been deducted.
Nineteenth hole	refers to the clubhouse bar.
Open tournament	open to both amateurs and professionals.
Out of bounds	areas on a course from which you may not play your ball. They are usually indicated by white markers.
Overclub	to hit the ball too far because you have taken the wrong club.
Overlapping grip	a style of holding the club.
Par	the number of shots a player should take to complete a hole or round.
Penalty stroke	a one-shot penalty a player must take for a rule infringement or for taking relief from an unplayable lie or hazard.
PGA	Professional Golfers' Association.

Pin . . . . .alternative name for the flagstick.
Pin high . . . . .a ball that has finished level with the hole as
. . . . .you look.
Play through . . . . .to allow players behind to overtake you.
Pot bunker . . . . .a small but steep sand trap.
Preferred lie . . . . .play where you can move your ball to a different
. . . . .spot no nearer the hole. Only permitted under
. . . . .certain conditions, such as winter rules.
Relief . . . . .picking up and dropping the ball without
. . . . .penalty and in accordance with the rules.
Rough . . . . .any area of high grass.
Sand trap . . . . .a hollow filled with sand.
Scratch player . . . . .a player so good no handicap is required.
Shank . . . . .to strike the ball off the part of the club where the
. . . . .club head meets the shaft.
Short game . . . . .chipping, pitching and putting.
Slice . . . . .a shot that goes sharp right in the air.
Stroke Index (SI) . . . . .ranking of a hole's difficulty. SI1 is the hardest
. . . . .hole on the course, SI18 the easiest.
Tee .peg on which ball is placed for tee shots. Also
. . . . .refers to the area from which tee shots are played.
Tee time . . . . .time at which you are scheduled to play.
Thin shot . . . . .a shot that goes along the ground because only
. . . . .the top half of the ball has been struck.

Underclub	.to hit the ball short of the target because you have taken the wrong club.
Wedge	.a type of club used to hit high shots into the green.
Winter rules	.local rules which are only applied in the winter.
Wood	.type of club used or long-range shots.
Yips	.a nervous condition which causes you to miss the simplest of putts.